ART OF THE IMPOSSIBLE

Books by Paul Hyland

POETRY

Riddles for Jack (Northern House, 1978)
Domingus (Mid-Day Publications, 1978)
Poems of Z (Bloodaxe Books, 1982)
The Stubborn Forest (Bloodaxe Books, 1984)
Kicking Sawdust (Bloodaxe Books, 1995)
Art of the Impossible: New and Selected Poems 1974-2004
    (Bloodaxe Books, 2004)

TRAVEL & TOPOGRAPHY

Purbeck: The Ingrained Island (Gollancz, 1978; Dovecote Press, 1989)
Wight: Biography of an Island (Gollancz, 1984; Dovecote Press, 1997)
The Black Heart: A Voyage into Central Africa
    (Gollancz, 1988; Henry Holt, 1989; Paragon House, 1990)
Indian Balm: Travels in the Southern Subcontinent
    (HarperCollins, 1994; Flamingo, 1995)
Backwards Out of the Big World: A Voyage into Portugal
    (HarperCollins, 1996; Flamingo, 1997)
Discover Dorset: Isle of Purbeck (Dovecote Press, 1998)

HISTORY

Ralegh's Last Journey (HarperCollins 2003; Flamingo 2004)

OTHER

Getting into Poetry (Bloodaxe Books, 1992; revised edition 1996)
Babel Guide to the Fiction of Brazil, Portugal and Africa,
    with Ray Keenoy and David Treece (Boulevard, 1995)

PAUL HYLAND

Art of the Impossible

NEW AND SELECTED POEMS 1974-2004

BLOODAXE BOOKS

ISBN: 1 85224 643 X

First published 2004 by
Bloodaxe Books Ltd,
Highgreen,
Tarset,
Northumberland NE48 1RP.

www.bloodaxebooks.com
For further information about Bloodaxe titles
please visit our website or write to
the above address for a catalogue.

Bloodaxe Books Ltd acknowledges
the financial assistance of
Arts Council England, North East.

Cover printing by J. Thomson Colour Printers Ltd, Glasgow.

Printed in Great Britain by
Cromwell Press Ltd, Trowbridge, Wiltshire.

CONTENTS

Domingus

Two poems for Lily Tilsley

ACKNOWLEDGEMENTS

This book consists of a body of new work together with poems selected from my earlier collections *Kicking Sawdust* (1995) and *The Stubborn Forest* (1984), as well as the complete text of *Poems of Z* (1982), all three titles published by Bloodaxe Books.

Thanks are due to the editors of the magazines, periodicals and anthologies in which many of these poems were first published. Since 1995 some have been included in the following books: *The Long Pale Corridor: contemporary poems of bereavement*, eds. Judi Benson and Agneta Falk (Bloodaxe Books, 1996); *Backwards Out of the Big World* by Paul Hyland (HarperCollins 1996); *The Bloomsbury Book of Love Poems*, ed. Benjamin Zephaniah (Bloomsbury, 1999); *Feelings*, ed. Fiona Waters (Longman, 2000); *The River's Voice*, eds. Angela King and Susan Clifford (Green Books, 2000); *Poems Then and Now*, ed. Fiona Waters (Evans, 2001); *Otter* (Common Ground, 2001); *Poems on the Underground*, eds. Gerard Benson, Judith Chernaik and Cicely Herbert (Cassell, 2001); *Everybody's Mother*, eds. Linda Coggin and Clare Marlow (Peterloo Poets, 2001); *Biscuits*, ed. Keiren Phelan (Southern Arts, 2001); *Land Writes*, eds. Paul Hyland and Helen Day (Artsreach, 2002); *The Honey Gatherers: a book of love poems*, ed. Maura Dooley (Bloodaxe Books, 2003); *Ochre and Ice* (Hart Gallery, 2003); and *Evidence* by Seán Street and Paul Hyland (Atrium Gallery, 2003).

Some poems were broadcast in the feature *Once-and-Future Portugal*, produced by Julian Hale (BBC Radio 3) and *The Radio 2 Arts Programme* (BBC Radio 2). The *Domingus* sequence, which originally sprang out of a collaboration with the printmaker Martin Ware, was produced for BBC Radio 3 by Fraser Steel and performed by John Franklyn-Robbins with a sound-score by the late Barry Anderson. *Poems of Z* was produced for BBC Radio 3 by Shaun MacLoughlin with the late, incomparable Maurice Denham as the spy-poet Z.

I thankfully acknowledge the following residencies and creative collaborations which catalysed, or bought time for, the writing of some of my recent poetry: Aldeburgh Poetry Trust, 1998; Write Up Your Street, Dorset Arts and Libraries, 1999; Subterranean Poetry, Poetry Society/Cleveland Arts Poetry Place, 1999; The Wall of Words, with letter-cutter Andrew Whittle and digital artist Kevin Carter, Dorset County Hospital, 2000; Trilith Year of the Artist radio project, Wiltshire, 2000-01; Otter, a new choral work with composer Helen Porter and Wimborne Community Theatre for Common Ground's Confluence project, 2001; Land Writes, with writer/editor Helen Day and photographer George Wright, Artsreach, 2002; Ochre and Ice, a catalogue and poems commissioned for an exhibition of Brian Graham's paintings at the Hart

Gallery, London, 2003; Evidence, an exhibition of paintings and prints by Brian Graham and Gemma Street with poems by Paul Hyland and Seán Street, the Atrium Gallery, Bournemouth University, 2003.

Special thanks are due to Pam Zinnemann-Hope, Zenobia Venner, Barry Tempest and Sue Hyland for their sustained critical encouragement.

The cover artwork by Ernst Thoutenhoofd draws on an Illinois Litho Co poster (*c.* 1931) advertising the Great Peters in Sells-Floto Circus.

To Make a Tree

Take wood, seasoned or green,
       rough-hewn or planed.
Take first one four-square beam
       twice a man's height,
then graft a second, half that,
       on to it,
cross-wise and near the top,
       cunningly joined.
Dig socket. Plant upright.
       Hope it will root,
hope sap will rise. If not,
       keep tools at hand
and, when the time is ripe,
       nail up the fruit.

SUBTERRANEAN POETRY

Iron and Steel

Son followed father
into the ironstone
paddling roadways and bords
in stiff new oil-soaked boots.

Pitch-black apprenticeship:
to be left by a trap listening
for your own blind breath
for wagons' thrum, hooves' clat

for the skinny bustle of rats
the skreak of stressed timber
the deep clout of a charge
and a far face tumbling

beginning a lifetime
of knowing that any night
he might go home alone
or you walk out an orphan.

Son follows father
into the steelworks,
from schoolyard and street
to thunder and hot sweat:

decanting gravity
and sun's fluorescence,
spooling earth's guts
out into the dull days.

If you should slip, slump
into molten steel, tenderly
he will place his boot
on your head and push you under.

Loftus Mine

There are small places and big places,
places in the rock that cleave clean

There is a narrow valley and open sea,
workings in seams that climb uphill

There are roadways, and mean refuges
to escape rattling tubs on the track

There's a ropeway and loading gantry
hefting ironstone to the steelworks

There is Skinningrove and there is Asia
and an old steelman's childish wonder

There's a train traversing pastel valleys:
steam between stumps of mountains

We made rails for China, he repeats,
rails for China, just imagine that

What was once under the ground just here
is in all manner of things all over

The Dimensions of Cleveland

1

Cliff land, tallest in the country:
harebells, heather, rusty rockface
over a quarried shelf where nothing
grows; ashen as aluminium
flushed angry pink, here, there,
with hints of calcined shale.

This ledge, blank and windblown
and high above a sea sprinkled
with ore-carriers and tankers,
held our first hellish industry:
clamps of rock and brushwood
fuming month upon month.

The stench, the leaching pits,
pans of green vitriol boiling
over coal fires, barrels of piss,
the smashed roaching casks,
the washings, hessian sacks full
of crystals: octahedral alum.

The world is more perfect
than our minds can imagine,
darker than our alum or jet
or ironstone mines can plumb.

2

Boulby, deepest in the country,
three-quarters of a mile down
through shales and rotten marl,
wet sandstone and mudstone
into dry heat, out under the sea
gnawing ochre potash, grey salt.

Remote-control creatures crawl
outwards along prehistoric
sea-beds, obeying geologists'
graffiti spray-painted on walls.
Behind them, men fire bolts up
to bond the ceiling's laminates.

Seven hundred miles of tunnels
but near the bottom of the shaft
a laboratory from which to look
further and more minutely
than before: shielded detectors
alert for WIMPS, for dark matter.

Weakly interacting massive particles
zap through the galaxy with no fuss
and all the gravitas they need
to hold the universe together.

3

You know the height and depth of it,
and the disputed length and breadth
of Cleveland, cliff-land stretched to fit
something more and less than itself,
claimed by landlords and Liègemen,
men of Dorset, and Cook, a Scotsman.

Stand on a cliff and own the horizon.
See the *Allomes Amye* out of Whitby,
master, Luke Fox, his stinking burthen
twenty-three tons of London urine
exchanged for twenty-eight of alum
to fix London colours in wool and linen.

In a drapers' shop, rub the bloom
off a South Sea Company shilling
between your finger and thumb,
flick it high in the morning sun
– heads, Staithes; tails, Australia –
beyond this county, both of them.

The long, imaginary shadow
of *Endeavour*, master, James Cook,
plays on the cliffs and slips away
to a country he can call his own.

Flying

A kestrel rides the updraft
above pigeons bustling out of lofts
high over narrow lanes in sharp grass
where fieldmouse, shrew and weasel go.
Windhover hangs above Skinningrove
hungry to stoop.

I stand at the valley's brink
stare down at the bird's rusty back
down onto mauled ground, flying high
over passages, tunnels, a criss-cross
subterranean world of bords and pillars
long since hewn out.

It is dusk and I could fall
into dreaming of the miners down there
women and bairns in their close rooms
cargoes of ironstone floating weightless
away from the jetty, or lightly steaming
zigzag uphill.

I could scan the pink ocean
or like the lad who revs his model plane
– fuselage gripped between his legs –
I could fly up and out of myself. Away.
At my back the steelworks sighs all night,
grinds like the sea.

Map of Abandonment
(Loftus Mines, closed 1958)

Pinned to the wall this fading map
shows a country few have entered
in forty years, a grid of roadways
and districts that might be a town

spread beneath hill, valley and cliff,
farmstead and pigeon-loft:
a map of what is not there
of what has been taken out.

A negative, where unworked
tracts hover like solid ghosts
under the church and graveyard,
consecrated and untouchable.

Every shift for a century
men disappeared under the hill
and Deepdale filled with spoil
till it was neither deep nor dale.

When the future crept up behind
them, the ironstone miners
walked from the drifts as usual,
drivers nuzzled their horses.

Men adjourned to club and pub
and glum home with a pound
for every year worked and a job
in the steel, or on the dole.

Some said, well, there'll be
no one maimed ever again,
no more deaths underground.
We could celebrate that.

Sure, men drank at the wake.
But only the horses went wild:
let into fields from dark lanes
and subterranean stables

to gambol in the huge dusk,
ungainly, wanton, crazily drunk
on freedom as if they sensed
no one would lead them back.

Rust haemorrhages down the beck
far beyond revelry or lament,
and pinned to the museum wall
is the old map of abandonment.

Cryptic

It could be a chapel
perched alone on Hunt Cliff
until we get close

its barrel-vaulted brick
its cement-clad tower
its emptiness

In the business of breath
that circular chamber
where the fan was

clogged shafts and gaping ducts
of an ironstone lung
the mine's Fan House

We squeeze inside and creep
its secret burrow for
a grope and kiss

nothing but undug ground
and a cliff-top railway
between sea and us

Here it's dangerous-safe
for sex and a smoke in
humid darkness

while on the loop of track
trains of potash or steel
throb as they pass

over emptied hills where
between Boulby and Tees
no one else breathes

Millennium

It's something like the end of a hard week
or a long day shift down the potash mine.
A glistening roof slithers above the truck
then bucks and dips close to our brimstone hats;
lamp-beams are bounced or sucked in by the dark.

10,000 lbs/in^2. Thick seas churn
a thousand metres up. We glide the shaft
and spill out into sunset. Stars, then dawn.
Too many big ideas have mucked us up.
Get in the cage. Get down to life, get down.

Richard Leycolt
('a workman from Purbeck, called Black Dick')

Where are you going, Dick?
North, I grunted. They said, Where north?
North Yorkshire, though it was hardly worth
naming a place that meant nothing.

I was glad to be gone from disputes,
for litigation had soured Dorset.
From Lord Mountjoy's lands I rode north
to John Atherton's grounds in Skelton
and found a place I knew in the earth,
a place in the rock, the dark shales,
a seam that was home to me.

Here I am mineral magus, chymist
who roasts rocks in earth-banked clamps;
greys and ochres blush brick-red.
Them I steep stage by stage in pits,
boil down a liquor, green vitriol.
We piss on it, tip tubs of urine in
from half the country, till it gives up
my elixir, the crystalline alum.

My men are sad dark creatures
in rags, sustained by poor victuals,
but what they get pleases farmers.
My mordant fixes colours in wool
off the moors, rich clothes and money.

Never enough. Soon they will sack me
for claiming more than I know,
more than I can perform or bring forth.
For now I know where I am, this north,
deep in it, its stench, its appetite.
And I wear it on my back.

The Love of Sea Creatures

Seal-pup at Saltburn

I am wary of men that smell unkind
and will not abide near them,
though often the women come down the sands,
to pluck shells at the tideline
laughing and singing their sea songs, hard hands
chucking me under the chin.

When one comes close, but silent in her skirts,
I see by her beard she's a man,
sense the weight of the stone in his basket
and know he will do me harm.
I am wrong, for he does not stun me but
like a prize carries me home.

I am young, with a place in his parlour,
a place in his affection;
I eat bread and milk and bask by the fire
or creep to lie close to him.
I cry when he throws me in the water
and nibble his toes again.

I was young, his home was mine.
Now he picks up and weighs stone after stone.

Mermaids at Staithes

Buffeted by big waves we made for shore,
fitful lights and boats below the Nab.
Later, I woke from tempestuous dreams
when my sister sang out, eyes wide and deep,
beached safe on the sands but circled around
by small eyes of women and men: fearful,
unquiet as the sea and more threatening.

We raised our hands and thrashed our tail-fins
but they grasped us under the arms and
dragged us to a lock-up between houses
where the sea was muffled and out of tune.
When we ailed they fetched us fish.
Boys and girls lunged at us through the bars,
plucked tresses, flicked pebbles at our breasts.

Come summer, they pitied us, wetted us,
let us out of our stench for a while:
whiles when we kept alert and waited,
when we squirmed to escape lewd fingers,
watching for solitude, for high tide,
for the day we flounder in, dive beyond
sticks or stones' reach and become ourselves.

I'll stand on my tail then, cry down a curse
that tempest take them house by house.

Sea-man of Skinningrove

Home is firm rock or sea that moves me,
though once I was tangled in what I'd not seen,
enmeshed in men's nets.

They skreaked at me and drew me ashore,
lifted me as though I should stand up like them,
dropped me on dry ground.

One house between cliffs being empty
they carried and settled me down in a room,
then spied round the door.

The bold ones stared, started when I flinched
or gazed into my eyes as I gaze in brine
to see my own face.

I ate none of meat, which they took back,
until fish was brought by some of the women
whom I looked long at.

I pleased the young women extremely,
liking how lustful and nervously brazen
they grew when we touched.

They left doors open. I came and went.
One day, secretly, I recovered my home
and swam swiftly out.

Men roar and rage and the women weep:
they have always adored me, but never known
how to perform it.

I rear myself up, in acknowledgement
of fair company and entertainment.

Cinders

(Carlin How, August 1999)

The furnace puts its molten tongue out
at the horizon, slobbers new cliffs
of slag and drools a road, once rail track,
down to a pier of concrete and rust;
the ultimate backdrop for romance,
a steelworks set high on a wrecked coast.

Its graveyard of weathered scrap iron
abuts the small church of St Helen's:
metaphorical graveyard, real church
like a drill hall with added steeple.
It's ready for a marriage made in
fairyland. In the sight of people.

It didn't look promising at first
but a pink coach topped with a gold crown
drawn by a pair of high-stepping greys
stopped at the works' fence. An excited
crowd videoed or snapped as the bride
in meringue and whipped cream alighted.

The coach's slender wheels crunch cinders,
the driver furls her whip, the golden
postillion adjusts a bra-strap,
and the sweet pageboy scratches his arse.
In church the bridegroom most likely sweats.
The bride's slippers are satin, not glass.

Her father arms her into the dark
bridesmaids and all, a flower-lit dream where
ritual deeds – learned vows and tongue-tied
signatures – will be too quickly done.
The world grows almost ordinary
till the couple step into the sun.

Above the sea, beside a steelworks
the plywood coach, plumes, gilt liveries,
frock-coats and white froth all edge towards
nostalgia's horizon, the future.
Fantasy winks, nudges transcendence.
The whole fucking pantomime's a prayer.

* * *

Young Lucie Comes to Tea

Young Lucie comes to tea
at her father's friends' house
with a snake up her sleeve.
She will enthral the ladies
and Janet, and Marianne.

To their alarm she pours
milk into her cupped palm
and lures the reptile out
to lap, before she slips
her rings off one by one.

It slides between the spoons,
flickers round plates and cups,
threads itself through each ring,
then coils, gathering them up
into a knot, a charm.

Grown-ups do not quite care
for this; for how they flinch
at hearing her declare,
When you ask me to dine
I'll braid him in my hair.

Memo concerning the Art of the Impossible

I will tell you my secret, which is that I have none.
We have our learning: techniques, methods, artifice
which we keep between ourselves, as being wasted
on the uninitiated, those who evince mere curiosity
not irresistible appetite; though if you crave miracles
you could not do worse than study the extravagance
of Crowley, colleague of the poets Yeats and Pessoa,
who honed self-worship, self-loathing needle-sharp;
you may profit from a study of the bank statements
of evangelists, cold readers, spoon benders, psychics
and the whole galaxy of self-promoting helpers who
make reputations from offering what cannot be had.

Or consider the career of the Great Peters, the man
with the iron neck who posed on a stage suspended
above a sawdust ring, then dropped seventy-five feet
with a hangman's noose slip-knotted about his neck:
an honest, death-defying feat, repeated and repeated
until one night not his spine, nor his legendary nerve
but his rope broke; a thrilled crowd saw him twitch,
lie still; his secret, miraculous or mundane, open or
occult, was lowered gently into the ground with him;
already he knows what you want to know, or nothing.

The Magus

(1st December 1947)

Within the shade of Netherwood,
a house screened by forbidding trees,
what burns in the Beast's rented room
fills it with sickly sweetness:
incense of Abra-Melin, the same
that ran down Aaron's beard.

At last the man in bed is impotent.
His thin moustache and goatee
twitch with the Word, 'Do what thou wilt
shall be the whole Law,' in a fussy
nasal voice that fades like a spilt
spell, cannot say where it went.

His signet ring asserts, 'His life
is in Khonsu,' moon god of Thebes
whose priest he was. But it is loose,
its circle cannot hold him, as his ribs
cannot hold up his lungs, and as
his heart cannot restrain its grief.

His wallet will bequeath to us
a parchment soaked in menstrual blood,
his calling cards – '*Sir* Aleister Crowley',
a cut-down diagram of the she-god
torn from a textbook of anatomy:
the vulva and – O, O! – the anus.

The heroin is high up on the shelf.
He has injected a last daily dose
of three or seven or eleven grains.
Shaking, 'I am perplexed,' the Logos
of the Aeon croaks his last sayings.
Last of all, 'Sometimes I hate myself.'

The Concertina in Its Cage

Then, it's so cruel easy! Oh, those tricks
That can't be tricks...
ROBERT BROWNING,
'Mr Sludge, the Medium'

He calls his squeezebox an accordion,
collapses it with a discordant yelp
and locks it in a cage beneath the table.
An afterlife is what it yearns.

He leans upon the table-top, eyes closed,
mouth shrouded by a soup-strainer
moustache, waiting with ears wide open
for angelic music's strains.

Now they come faint and thin.
The sound's ethereal, and it is true
his toes, confined in lace-up boots,
don't dance the concertina's buttons.

Reedy cacophony resolves itself
first into *Home, Sweet Home* then
wheezes *The Last Rose of Summer*.
Heaven loves banal nine-note tunes.

You have to believe it. An eminent
physicist observes the séance
in the full glare of electric light.
There is no other explanation.

The concertina in its cage
appears inert, and yet imbued with airs
returning from beyond the grave,
so sentimental and so human.

The medium seems to lick his lips,
tonguing a miniature harmonica
into one cheek, then opens up
his occult mouth to say Amen.

MILLSTRODE

Millstrode Was Born

Millstrode was born with an open mind
long hair, no teeth, and a soul
(he had no confidence in it, it
was grey and slippery), and time:
roughly five hundred and thirty
thousand hours of it to spend
and waste and lose (he also sold
around a hundred thousand cheap
to a succession of men with money).
Meanwhile, it must be added
his hair fell out and grew again
his teeth grew and fell out and
grew once more, then his hair fell
out and his teeth and his soul.

Millstrode Descendant

Millstrode, now grand with lather,
takes time off shaving to invent
a fake and rugged father
for himself: a fat tycoon,
flamboyant gambler, sleuth
or hairy tramp with eyes
bright as his useful teeth.

Millstrode licks soapy lips, sighs,
spits and dreams; anyone but
the father whose he is,
the toothless employee, the shade
he daily grows to recognise
unmasked by a blunt blade.

Millstrode's Götterdämmerung

Millstrode is jealous of the children
he never had. Sometimes he wishes his
had been the last birth cord they cut.
Ad nauseam he tells the joke about
posterity: What of it then?
What has it ever done for us?
He sips his double scotch and sees
his lost, last goddam generation
engulfed to here in global orgies.
A glorious götterdämmerung!
No cares, duties to anyone,
nothing conserved or spared. Fuck it,
we'd suck the planet to a prune,
exhaust the blasted world of joys,
then put a damn bomb under it,
goodbye old man. Sometimes he's serious.

Millstrode, Iconoclast

Out on the moor
Millstrode jumped
on God's granite feet.

On a stool in the bar
Millstrode stood,
strangled God
hands trembling with power,
God's juice
running his taut wrists
like sweat.

Millstrode's Friends

Some of his friends have come.
Today he don't want friends
but introduces, sets them
at each other's throats, and stands
absent in bulk while they get on with it.
They get on well. He smothers
yawns and plans tomorrow's visits.
To set each right about the others.

Millstrode Cuts Short His Holiday

Just like at home he walked abroad at dusk
but he'd forgot how many stars there were,
how many scents hung in the wooded air.
He felt the faint dew dropping on his hair
and heard the cattle cud, or tug at grass.
He had forgot how self-sufficient these,
the trees and bedded rocks were. He, a husk.

That first week of his annual holiday
the sun shone as it used to on the world;
but Millstrode's clement weather could not hold,
he sickened bad for home and had to shield
his eyes till blinding headlights sliced the air
for miles and merged snug with the city's glare,
his stirring soul restored, to memory.

Millstrode's Next Resort

Millstrode resorts to crowded coasts
where well-oiled bodies all on heat
lie quite abandoned on the sands
and warm each other variously.

In such close comfort Millstrode roasts,
breathes life, the seaweed's healthy rot,
chuckles at freaks and fitness fiends
and big girls' ebb and flow at sea.

Then if he dreams that all these hosts,
trudged to the edge, must rock the boat,
upset the shore, that scores of hands
dabble with water as they die...

he gulps awake, shakes head and hastes
to take his second option out:
to lie, abandoned on the sands,
and stare into a crowdless sky.

*   *   *

Spirit from the Forest
(Yakusu, Congo)

I am a white man who has strayed
    by choice into a forest
The whole world is a settlement
    hedged about by the forest
The village flares with eyes and fires –
    darkness lives in the forest
Night-and-day and life-and-death look
    contrary in the forest
My dugout draws a fluid stitch
    between forest and forest
The talking drum's lips, thick and thin
    speak of me to the forest
Pronounce my name to the far bank
    as 'spirit from the forest'
To those eyes I've the pallor of
    ancestors from the forest
My eyes the colour of the eyes
    of big cats in the forest
I ask for the respect I give
    the people of the forest
But because drums can only speak
    as they speak in the forest
And eyes can only shy away
    from pale eyes in the forest
I'm given a part I can't play in
    the darkness of the forest
Returned into the world I am
    the spirit from the forest
It's hard to enter life, to be
    reborn out of the forest

Lament
(Lusengo, Congo)

Ah, mama Ewoyo, you are cold.
There will be buyers for your dried fish
For your smoked monkey, but no seller:
Ah, mama Ewoyo, you are cold.

By my bed a mantis prayed all night
And my sweat flowed like the great river;
By yours, traders spread their hands and wailed:
Ah, mama Ewoyo, you are cold.

At dawn canoes came, fought our bow-wave
To make fast, with kwanga, crocodile,
But your stock needs no replenishing:
Ah, mama Ewoyo, you are cold.

Beside a forest village we moored,
Gave money towards your funeral;
A man swung an adze, others dug deep:
Ah, mama Ewoyo, you are cold.

A woman with heavy breasts, grass skirt
Walked round the hole, a soldier watched
Your raw box borne by many hands:
Ah, mama Ewoyo, you are cold.

At the top of the Congo's great bend
Half a day, then rattles, chants and prayers
And a spade passed strong arm to strong arm:
Ah, mama Ewoyo, you are cold.

Ah, mama Ewoyo, you are cold.
There will be buyers for your dried fish
For your smoked monkey, but no seller:
Ah, mama Ewoyo, you are cold.

The Bell

(Oradour-sur-Glane)

We wake to church bells' frantic discipline.
That morning, though, the tocsin should have rung.
Bell-metal does not rust like any old iron.

Today it is the brown corroded things
in barns and garages and roofless homes
that seem so ineradicably human:

each tool, car, bicycle and sewing-machine
decays little by little until worn
almost away by weather and by time.

So quickly the forgettable remains
were burnt; near the bullet-scarred altar stone
in church, rests the charred chassis of a pram.

Oh, that morning the tocsin should have rung.
By dusk the tower's molten bell had fallen.
It squats here still, an overripe bronze plum.

La Covadonga

On the restaurant wall
in her shrine stands Nuestra Señora
scarlet virgin of battles.
She is the only detail
almost out of place among dark oak
perfect mirrors and white linen.

At a well-appointed table
near the door to the kitchen
sits Rosa Gimenez Moreno
the swarthy one, the wily
peasant who knows how to please,
gulping her own good food.

Rosa's suave son, side-burns
a shade too long, presides
at the bar over breakages
uncorkings, dispensing of shots
doing almost nothing himself
almost classy like one of the Family.

Rosa's sturdy granddaughter
purple hair shimmering
short mauve skirt riding up
serves me like she cares
while her grandmother smiles
while her uncle almost sneers.

While unseen cooks grimace
over knives and pans and stoves
fabada and *trucha con jamón*,
the door between heaven and earth
is buffeted to and fro and I
am almost inclined to say grace.

The Leaves' Audible Smile
(after Fernando Pessoa)

The leaves' audible smile
is no more than the breeze over there.
If I look at you and you look at me,
who is the first one to smile?
The first to smile laughs.

Laughs, and looks suddenly,
with the idea of not looking,
at where they sense in the leaves
the sound of the wind passing.
All is wind and dissembling.

But that look, from looking
where it does not look, turned;
and the two of us are talking
of what was unspoken.
Is this ending or begun?

Sorriso audível das folhas,
Não és mais que a brisa ali.
Se eu te olho e tu me olhas,
Quem primeiro é que sorri?
O primeiro a sorrir ri.

Ri, e olha de repente,
Para fins de não olhar,
Para onde nas folhas sente
O som do vento passar.
Tudo é vento e disfarçar.

Mas o olhar, de estar olhando
Onde não olha, voltou;
E estamos os dois falando
O que se não conversou.
Isto acaba ou começou?

For Pero Moniz, who died at Sea

(a version, after Luís de Camões)

On earth I lived few years, and weary ones,
cram-full of stubborn, wretched misery;
the dark day's light deserted me so soon
I never saw my quarter century.

I travelled across far-off lands and seas
seeking some remedy for life, some cure;
but daring deeds do not bring happiness
to one who, finally, has no desire.

Portugal bred me in my dear and green
homeland of Alenquer; but corrupt air
trapped in my vessel, in this blood and bone,

made me a morsel for your fish, cruel
sea, breaking on barren Abyssinia
so distant from my fertile native soil.

No mundo, poucos anos e cansados
vivi, cheios de vil miséria dura;
foi-me tão cedo a luz do dia escura
que não vi cinco lustros acabados.

Corri terras e mares apartados,
buscando à vida algum remédio ou cura;
mas aquilo que, enfim, não quer ventura,
não o alcançam trabalhos arriscados.

Criou-me Portugal na verde e cara
pátria minha Alenquer; mas ar corruto,
que neste meu terreno vaso tinha,

me fez manjar de peixes em ti, bruto
mar, que bates na Abássia fera e avara,
tão longe da ditosa pátria minha!

La Virgen con el niño escribiendo en un libro

The Virgin

is the usual kind:
blue–cowled
serene
infinitely concerned
with God
oddly fulfilled

The Child

is the usual kind:
four months old
his middle–aged
forehead
plump with purpose
that can't be framed

The Writing

is not the usual kind:
ink leaking
onto paper
from a pen
in the child's hand
not so much letters
as formulae
of an alchemist
an Einstein

The Book

is the usual painted kind
whose pages can't be turned
or shut

Back to Tordesillas, 1494

Retrospect is easier.
From my table in the plaza

I gaze at old men gazing,
spitting, gossiping, smoking.

Before me is a photocopy,
reduced, of the old treaty

weighed down by a glass of wine
and a rearguard sense of doom.

That it was signed in this town
seems improbable, is certain.

What would you call my failure
to get inside the Holy Father's

skull, into the heads of kings
who sealed this with their rings?

They scored a line of longitude
pole to pole through suspected

but unseen South America.
They had new worlds to share

or, rather, split between them.
Mine is a hopeless question.

They would call mine a failure
of imagination. Sure.

Present
(Valencia)

Like shoes in lighted shops, time comes in sizes.
At dusk bats catapult themselves between church
pinnacles and up façades of banks. A girl in black

hangs out down on the pavement, knees at her ears,
arms folded round her shins, hands stretching for
the finger-holes of her bone-white recorder.

Perhaps a tune trickles behind one open eye
but breath barely escapes her lips. She plays a sigh,
narrow and deep as silence where bats flit.

In the elastic moment that is twilight
she pipes a squeak and stalls, keels over like a kite.
Shoes clatter past her head as the clocks strike.

* * *

Good Money

The money is good and
of course it makes him happy.
He e-mails and makes calls;
he keeps an eye on indices;
he chooses his moments;
he networks and lunches
lightly on divine morsels
and water, which fuel the small
movements he makes to make
money. He lives in the real
world. The men who built
the pyramids did the same.

Diagrams, graphs, arithmetic.
The money is good and
naturally it makes him happy.
No doubt their money also
bought them secretary/PAs
who remembered birthdays
and anniversaries and ordered
gifts and flowers, the minutiae
of life kept in place with no
discernible effort. His girl
books tickets and personal
services; renews subscriptions

to journals, exclusive clubs,
and to the executive gym
where three times a week
he pushes his tireless body
to shift meaningless weight,
to run directionless miles,
to shed deodorised sweat and
the small surplus he does
not want. He's made it,
made everything he has,
made himself what he is
today. Life is tough but

the money is good and,
sadly, it makes him happy.

P(r)aying for Dinner

(for Ian Duhig)

What does the scrollwork spell
on your *Diner*'s plastic?
Who weighs wisdom against wealth,
or illumination against
figures scratched on vellum?

Offa the Mercian, the mercenary
balances his books, strikes
pence like Frankish *deniers*;
designs on his gold coins
mimic the Caliph's *dinars*.

Coin words ignorantly,
let christian Offa be embraced
by this voluptuous text:
There is no God but one,
Mahomet is his prophet.

Text

The hermit
Haji Wali Muhammad
dreamed his mission,

dedicated his life
to gathering damaged
and discarded pages.

He pushes open
a heavy iron door
into a hole in the hill,

a labyrinth
of tunnels penetrating
the mountain above Quetta

where with his acolytes
he stores 65,000 sacks,
pillow-cases, plastic bags

full of spoiled scripture
out of the sun. The air is dry,
cool and scented with cloves.

The word of Allah
must never be destroyed.
The hermit heaves it, hoards it

for the long winter,
the afterlife, eternity
in his catacombs.

Lightly he touches it,
blessed indeed to gaze upon
tonnes of paper he cannot read.

Prester John

I have left my kingdom
three days' march
from earthly paradise:
full of stones, both precious
and magical, psychic
animals and rare plants
with healing attributes;
a place of harmony
and, need I say it, peace;
at the holy mount's foot
we drink the soft waters
of everlasting youth
from a transparent source.

I ride from that kingdom
at the head of armies;
with them I aim myself
at far-off holy wars
in a holy land where
we go to reinforce
and replace crusaders;
we have gained the left bank
of the river Tigris
but find we cannot cross;
now I have waited years,
always hoping that next
winter the waters freeze.

Childermas

Enjoy your Christmas sitting by the fire
replete with interactive fantasy,
eyes flickering but focused on screen where
warriors brandish blades and victims flee.
There's little fear of an angelic choir
to break the wintry silence. Press a key:
relish your first night huddled in a byre
before you learn to be a refugee.

Out of this world it is, an unreal toy
better than TV news or old pretence:
for every three wise guys who come with joy
and gifts of gold and myrrh and frankincense
out of the east to greet the glory boy,
one Herod slaughters many innocents.

Tethered

The world is boy-sized, girl-sized, anywhere.
Outside I watch my old one, thumbnail-small,
but swivel from the sight of that blue ball
to tweak controls upon the fascia.

Like pillow talk, a soft voice crackles 'Go!'
I check suit, airlock, oxygen before
I move: the kid who waited by the door
to be pushed out into unearthly snow.

Slowly I tumble, tethered by a cord
that links umbilicus to high-tech womb.
I work at solar cells on the dark side
but long to cut free, slide into the dream:
those laden pines, that snowfield blank and wide,
this wish to run away but not leave home.

On the Hook

The phone rings and, offhand, you answer it
as if you'd not been waiting here for this.
But this is all that holds you to her now:
alarms, the sudden calls, second-hand cries
that stir the dregs of love somewhere in you
where she can bear them, being out of sight.

You listen hard to what your daughter says
fresh from her mother's bed in hospital;
you barely thank her, *Ta love*, and ring off.
She's drying out in casualty for now,
you say, *there's no point visiting tonight,*
and add at once, as if it was required,

She's still under sedation, there's no point.
And then, as if it was the only way
to answer such alarms, and not a trick
you've learnt from years of it out of your hands,
you slowly straighten up, and step outside.
Leave the receiver sleeping on the hook.

Eurhythmics

Born premature, less than three pounds,
late to eat, to speak, to walk,
you've stumbled somehow ever since.

Now, dressed like Isadora, you dance,
your entranced face younger
than your long hands reaching out

past failure. You talk about that:
hard birth, failed school, bad health,
jobs held for a day or less.

Fluent, you speak of your one success
way back, smallholding somewhere
between Hamilton and Auckland

where you reared orphan lambs by hand,
fed them every two hours
awake for a week, the dream-time

nuzzling, nurturing spare warmth
in the dawn to wean them
from you, and at last to sleep.

Here, in your floating white, you keep
the temper of the dance, hands slack
then reaching out, forward and back.

Clenched

The baby's crying scours her brain-pan clean.
Massive tears bud from his clenched lids and course
stainlessly down onto the sheet, or drain
into the awful void behind her eyes.

She smacks the boy quite hard, quite hard enough.
He gags and summons shrieks out of a place
much bigger than himself, that drive her deaf
and fill her head with his distorted face.

Her lover's footfalls thud upon the stair.
He snatches him. His child, her child abuse.
But will he understand her, her hoping
for something not unkind and not unfair
to curb not cause uncalled-for wretchedness,
to keep at least one part of her from weeping?

Snowman Song
(London SW12)

Pavement full of footfalls,
and more than broken glass
glistens on tops of walls,
lies like dung in gutters.

Beneath street lights, the quiet
broken by two small boys
excited and out late,
grubbing white off the grass.

Her hair like oiled darkness,
their mother risks the road
to catch her runaways,
her sari swathed in tweed.

The verge's meagre quilt
rolled up into a mass:
snow-god the night sky spilt
who'll stand marooned for days.

Somerfield

So this is paradise.
A boy picks gleaming apples
from a bottom supermarket shelf
and lobs them into the top one,
Gala to Cox's. Some fun.

A poor aim and the laws
of physics insist most fall
at shoppers' feet or roll between
trolley-wheels. Much muttering
about control and discipline.

What else but practice can
improve him? His mother
stands across the aisle selecting
aubergines. Yes, she would give
anything to teach him to live.

Like screams and beatings
in the orchard when our gang
was captured scrumping pippins
from grey trees. Or lucky falls,
narrow escapes over high walls.

This boy's calm mum moves on
to dairy produce, Eden Vale.
Ignore him. No sin's original.
Sometimes exotic fruit boxes make
nests for spiders. Rarely a snake.

Rehabilitation Centre

The men in this prefabricated hut
survived at least two wars and qualified
for second childhood here – where they are taught
to cope with life, with tasks that earn their keep –
by virtue of arthritis, age or seizure.

Unfailing minds fixed on the model kits
their slow hands are contracted to pack up:
tanks, planes and boats, boxed plastic bits
designed to be dismembered and rebuilt
by nimble-fingered children at their leisure.

Die

When he died
the doctor did not
use the opaque word.

She did not say
Your father has died,
or, Your father is dead.

Die as a verb
is too final perhaps;
as a noun too chancy.

She did not say
Your father has stopped,
packed up, like a clock.

She did not say
He has come apart
and can't be mended.

Nor did she say
ceased, from which word
there is no return.

What she said was,
Your father has gone.
I'm sorry, he's gone.

Which led you to ask,
Where? And afterwards,
How can I join him?

Springing My Mother

Tonight my mother asked my niece
for the key of the house, because
later I am to arrive like a visitor
at her hospital bed and guilelessly
chat as my lover empties the locker
and smuggles her things to the car.

Then, while the nurses are fully
preoccupied with tea and chatter,
I am to commandeer a wheelchair
and push her down the long corridor
in my softest shoes, into the world.
Every angle has been considered.

It will be as if my mother has died.
My niece, coming home, will find her.
Doctors, bemused by our boldness,
will gaze at the empty bed, at the void
in her cupboard. Sister will shake out
the bolster that passed a peaceful night.

I am not sure we'll get away with it
but I muse on Colditz and George Blake.
I wish I had had more time to consider
the pratfalls. I cannot help myself laughing.
The first I heard of tonight's master plan
was my incredulous niece on the phone.

In Chittlehampton Churchyard

1

Nine months have gone since we threw handfuls of
clay-loam and shale on to the coffin lid;
the earth has settled in my father's grave.
Reuben and I have come with spades to bed

the headstone in: unweathered warm Thornback,
one cut and lettered face, delivered from
Treleven's quarry on the cliffs of Purbeck.
Reuben thinks he must dig, but I am firm;

no appetite for tears, only for toil,
for planting Dorset stone in Devon soil.

2

Since we stood here twenty-one years have passed;
today we've come simply to lift a turf
and tip these ashes in, our mother's dust.
We feel twice over and remember love.

We speak. It's a light task, hardly more than
a gesture, made to link lives long parted.
A chisel will soon stutter at the stone,
dust will fall, to mark the place we started.

The slab will hold an added name and date,
this little plot bear more than twice the weight.

Back of the Stone
(Heptonstall)

Thickset stone
with deep-cut lettering
SOPHIA 2 years 3 months.
Her followers:
a brother in his thirtieth year
ALSO her father
ALSO her mother.

Verso
light chisel strokes, austere,
voluptuous as Venus rising
or Sophia through clouds:
blown drapes and braids
neat breasts
a naive face.

Conviction's secretive caress
solidly named
AN ANGEL IN HEAVEN
trumpeting like a glass-blower:
a bubble, the music of
a crystal sphere,
the crystal sea.

Ararat

So now the ark has bumped aground once more
and we two disembark on Ararat

an island peak that shrugs the waters off,
swells slowly to encompass all the world

peopled and hectic, full of heady trash
as well as what we care for recklessly.

But always in our heads we hold that hull,
an aromatic darkness where we breathe

new airs and find ourselves again, life-size,
within such confines as we cannot plumb.

Wedding Song

(St Aldhelm's Chapel)

This is a wishing-place,
a house from which to start,
stone hut on a headland
jutting seaward and skyward
above the tumbling sea.

We step into the dark,
gaze at two figures poised
above the depth and weight
of rocks land-slipped and tumbling
above the tumbling sea.

The pillar's stoup for charms
draws us towards the heart
where the dance happens
between falling and rising,
above the tumbling sea.

Be still. Be still: centre
yourselves on the edge
of the future; take a breath
together and step out
above the tumbling sea.

Katherine

(Abbotsbury)

When I first saw you in the glass
pale, insubstantial Katherine
I did not know whose ring you wore;
I hardly saw your halo's fire
the wheel of spikes which you endure
the block to which you have to walk.

Now when I catch you in the glass
gazing beyond this leaded pane
I note a soft mouth, two frank eyes
– beauty that's Alexandria's –
the long line of a noble nose
and clasped hands lapped by golden silk.

The candle burning at the glass
dims what I see, tough Katherine:
I glimpse you whole who knew the stakes
and barely flinched beneath the axe.
The flame is bloody but the wax
runs down as light becoming milk.

Boy with Frying-pan
(Lyme Regis)

A boy ran home to fetch a frying-pan.
Neighbours,
                    a crowd of them, saw
waves not lapping but licking at the cliff
and beach like flames.
                              None would forget
that vision, how at eight on a misty night
for that boy
                    waves *were* flames of fire,
a fact he wanted to hold in both hands
as the rest looked on.
                              He took the pan
and dipped it in and lifted it up, shining,
and tipped it onto the ground:
                                        sea water
falling through air, splashing off stones,
spitting like sparks
                    as if the elements
could be changed at will in the grasp
of a boy
                    who next morning would hear
how across the bay the spew and spate
of his inferno seemed
                              like lightning.
Like sheltered everyone from the sight,
and from the boy
                    who crept back home
to set the pan on ashes in the grate.

54

Otter

High in the dusk
I stand on a bridge,
bats like shuttles
flinging invisible
nets beneath arches.

Something pops
the river's membrane:
black snout, flat head,
fluted fur streaming,
a disappearance.

The surface heals
and slides downstream,
my eyes alert
for the place, the next
door out of the deep.

As long as I search
it will not open;
my cars straining
at thin air for a plop,
a chirp, a whistle.

Nothing breaks
surface or silence;
still, I am drawn into
its element, this last-light
luminescence,

the web and flux
of worlds contained
in jet eyes, waiting
for a skinful of gold,
a naked whisker.

Discontinuity

Under the filigree hill
a man in a breathy cloud
bends with a bucket
between two pale horses.

The planet's thin skin
– usually duplicitous
and shifty – this morning
is frozen, silent,
fragile and solid.

An antique pewter hedge
between a high-walled yard
and a stiff farmhouse
is pierced by a black hole
I have not noticed before:

a man-sized aperture,
a shadow in the rime
where this morning no one climbs
the low hedge bank,
ducks through foliage
and disappears.

Nothing moves through it but years.

OCHRE AND ICE

for Brian Graham

Dig

Downland. Incised chalk.
Pots, flints and flint cores.
An inhumation. Ashes;
and, like the resurgence of
long-buried dreams, hares,
muscle-bound and lithe,
throb across earth's skin
with shadow-tipped ears.

Evidence

Not always obvious
it is what shows up
in taciturn hearths or pits
when we look hard.

It comes of seeing:
noticing something
out of the and utterly
ordinary

that has not faded
from the skimpy soil
or been digested by
oblivion.

Not often a crime
but mostly a wrong:
some outrage or disease
that scars the bone.

Something just fallen
or deliberately placed
and left, either way, to
posterity.

Appetite and need.
Scant evidence of love
except you lying there,
me standing here.

Prehistory

(Oakdale)

Deep river, flood water breaches the mind;
the garden stream, dammed up, pools a great lake
in a landscape of lawn, stones, sandy soil
and shadowy flower-bed forests. Like
any small boy you live in a big world.

Crack a stone open: creamy shell, then yolk
of a blue-grey that jumps you above clouds
or dunks you under sea; knap the flint – *thok*,
insistent *thok* – to axe, tower, headland,
sometimes a graphic glimpse of man, horse, deer.

Sparks fly between struck stones, quick metaphors,
flashes of pigment that advance, retreat,
bridges between harmonious opposites
where, on the brink of the impossible,
we live bare-faced and open-eyed, in awe.

When chickenpox confines you to your room
you stare at workmen come to plumb your stream
through pipes, back-fill and drive it underground.
Too old to cry, you will wait years to find
the hidden *source*, a trickling pipe in France.

A glacier melts in Bournemouth, so you make
for Hengistbury Head's scoured sanctuary.
Dig it now, slice it, taste it. Here you are
in your bed, warm as crumpets, rich as cake.
Fire in the hearth dies. Pick charcoal and draw.

Floorplan
(Culverwell)

In sea or lake, soil or sediment
some things sink
beyond our digging while others surface
in the slant light.

A reindeer carcase weighted with rocks
drifts down, down;
all our games and jokes, tales and rituals
fall through the cracks.

The remains of what we have lived off,
the midden,
is paved over with what we have lived on:
the limestone floor.

The bed of stones glints: shards of a pot
or a skull
from which everything tender has seeped
into the dirt.

Hell Stone
(Portesham)

See how the tall stones lean together,
how each one kisses the capstone,
how the glorious body is laid within
accoutred and accompanied by wealth.

Watch how the boulders and flat stones
are heaped up, how earth is tamped down
to make the hollow hill where a king sleeps.
When I see the green mound I will recall this.

But I dreamt it naked, saw it stripped bare,
the kissing stones a sieve for the wind,
the hill's womb empty; and in the dream
I knew myself too to be unremembered.

Nostalgic Study in Crayon
(Hengistbury Head)

If the world was relatively undisturbed
we could gather its components and fit them
back together. With flint artefacts found here
we can play that game after twelve thousand years:
puzzle tools and flakes back on to their cores.

The hunters had to make a round trip
of fifteen miles to fetch nodules of this size,
unless merchants travelled here to trade
flint for Hengistbury crayon: clay stained
with brown or red or bright pink ferric oxide.

If only the world had been undisturbed;
and if we could only un-draw the ochre
sketches on rock, smudges on human skin,
reel back intention on to the crayon, and on,
and wilfully draw, draw, draw it out again.

Original

If we dig here
between the two rivers
Tigris and Euphrates
we must come up
with something good:

A stratified trench,
trowel and brush work
inching a route back
to the detonation
of *homo sapiens*.

At bottom, knowledge
and life: two fossil trees
whose petrified heartwood
is zealously dated
to zero hour.

Concentric rings uncoil,
bend and unbend like
a serpent's subtle bones
in the primeval soil,
a humanoid rib.

No place for a woman,
this, or man, a garden
of earthly delights
undermined and carpeted
by ignoble savages.

A fertile wilderness,
furrows and craters
impregnated with toxins,
shells, bombs and corpses
of the late Holocene.

Quadrat

The frame's a quadrat
laid upon the earth
to mark the boundaries
of a sample plot:

strata of paint built up
with sand and filler,
to be scored through
and excavated back.

The frame's a window
looking in, or out
of a deep cave at noon,
a lit room in blank night;

an occult mirror,
or an open door which
limits what we see,
enlarges vision.

Forensic

The story seeps away
with the soothing rain
over a threshold
that once had meaning,
down to the stream.

All her clothing decays;
fibre and leather rot
to mulch and mix
with the leaf-mould
floor's clean stench.

Her body, long since
a bloated big top
for bacillus and fungus,
is struck and secreted
amongst the elements.

Her bones feed neither
fox nor wolf but lie
alone under the clouds
under the shade of trees
under herb and hedge

beneath all the layers
the years spread out,
quilt upon downy quilt
over her, until she is
more than forgotten.

His flesh also is hidden
that held and impaled her
with something like love.
Only his weapon of flint
loses none of its edge.

Elemental Properties

Scrimshaw

Rib of cow
hand of man
tool of desire
speed of horse

Knap

Heart of flint
hammer of horn
arrows of air
pluck of song

Lookout

Ladder of sticks
swell of horizon
herd of deer
stomach of knives

Cure

Hair of beast
edge of scraper
touch of skin
cloak of silence

Hearth

Ring of stones
web of limbs
suck of fire
blab of tongues

Flint

Blot of light
glimpse of darkness
blade of stone
gift of death

Grave

Arena of nought
cave of meal
hoard of things
ark of dreams

Bridge

String of steps
destroyer of space
end of stride
start of worlds

Tent

Belly of skin
ribs of wood
bag of secrets
bed of self

Headland

Jaw of rock
tongue of earth
words of wind
sight of beyond

*   *   *

Ovid Plastering

To be candid
it's better than sentry duty
in the unspeakable Black Sea winter

Do not believe
all you read in my *Tristia*
though my hand is cold on this wet trowel

The masonry
provincial but sound enough
a bed for my apprentice upward strokes

The art of love
must be renounced reluctantly
only when *Remedia Amoris* fail

In far Rome once
I saw Virgil but didn't speak
regrets unaccountable and precious

It's not prison
this room I am making a world
choosing to live where fate has exiled me

I like the thought
of wet gypsum's blank expanses
after some practice I'll love the finish

With a damp brush
and steel I burnish it bone-white
then paint on it endlessly with my mind

I watch it dry
patchily like the beach or clouds
changing and changing into perfection

Bicycles
(at Oradour-sur-Glane 1994)

There is no more useless thing
than a twisted bicycle,
unless it's two of them hung
from one nail in the wall:

three warped wheels
a necklace of rusty chain
a crossbar and four pedals
like rudimentary limbs,

crankshaft locked solid
with fifty years' weather
beyond the blaze that shrugged
off tiles and lifted rafters.

Exposed, these bicycles
are frail and wiry, faintly
human mechanicals
half gone, linked gently

  pedals to feet
handlebars to hands
saddle to seat –
by nothing more than

memories, useless ones
of that summer afternoon
when the inhabitants
were herded to the green,

men into barns, women
and children into church;
this place an empty lane
an overcrowded ditch.

Near Guernica

My teeth meet through a thick tortilla
inside the café of deep silence
on the road to Miranda de Ebro.

The coffee is darkest Arabica
tilted at narrow whispering faces,
the blood most likely of group O

and Rhesus negative. Men's boiler
suits are plangent blue, shirts sonorous
grey, somewhere a secretive radio

and in relief on the wall, Guernica,
carved and burnished woodwork that owes
everything but beauty to Picasso.

The lightbulb has a warm patina,
the hybrid bull glows, the screaming horse
is a well-polished palomino.

I am eating food off an altar,
gazing at an unholy reredos
with peaked flames instead of a halo.

Here, where strangeness is familiar
the sword snaps, the turned lamp gutters
and today's long-buried voices grow

suddenly raucous. Workmen's laughter
lifts words, music from the Caucasus
perhaps, from the east and long ago.

Picture of Nobody
(El Salvador)

A picture full of women and
one man in a picture in the picture.
One woman holds the frame but
we cannot see her hands
we cannot see the lap
that bears the man, the icon.

Next to her a comrade hides
her eyes with a bent hand.
Behind her the women grow
indistinct, massed, as if miles
of women pressed up to the lens
this focus, this man whose eyes

fix us. The others cast down.
Here is sorrow, anguish, outrage
he is not part of. He is absent
is disappeared, he is the man
child slipping from the grasp
of the angry, mourning virgin.

* * *

Dom Sebastião, King of Portugal
(after Fernando Pessoa)

Mad, yes, mad, for I wanted majesty
such as Fate never allows.
My conviction did not fit within me;
that's why, where the desert lies
my has-been self remained, not he who is.

My madness, let others take it from me
and all that went with it.
Without madness what can man be
other than a healthy brute,
a postponed corpse that procreates.

Louco, sim, louco, porque quis grandeza
Qual a Sorte a não dá.
Não coube em mim minha certeza;
Por isso onde o areal está
Ficou meu ser que houve, não o que há.

Minha loucura, outros que me a tomem
Com o que nela ia.
Sem a loucura que é o homem
Mais que a bestia sadia,
Cadáver adiado que procria?

The Tradition of Discovery

(Costa Nova, Portugal)

How the breakers muster force
from the Atlantic's breadth.
This gravitas between continents
weighs upon a lost land-mass
booms and sighs in the long sands
like dreams that lift, shrug, overtake sleep.

The sun voyages westwards, its aura
highlights everything's edges: this shore
a strand between river and sea,
footing for the precarious town,
its young poised on the margin.
Two are posed, now, in the surf's lace.

The white floes of her dress and veil
wash around, between, the darker legs
of his dark suit. They embrace,
leap and laugh at the big waves.
Their wedding flowers burn in the sun
and, doused, glisten with brine.

These moments the photographer takes;
his tripod's legs lapped in foam bear
the scene's weight, the still edge, the timeless
flowers. Two, close and shining. Between,
a sun, an ocean. The shutter's snick
discovers a continent rising.

Loquat Song

O the loquats Rosalinha
    plucks me from her backyard tree,
Teeth must try, and find their skins are
    taut and tart and tempting me.

How the flesh bursts on my palate,
    how the juice burns on my tongue.
Laughs Rosalinha – You must wait! –
    so I wait, too long, too long.

Her thick legs and crop-soiled fingers
    are decked out in black, in black;
On her lips a girl's smile lingers,
    lover's lustre in her look.

While beneath the stern green foliage
    fruit grows golden with the sun,
My plucked loquats die of old age,
    brown and wrinkled, on the wane.

But I mouthe a sour-plum, split her
    and am ravished with delight.
When they're ripened, O how bitter,
    when they're rotten, O how sweet

Like men's souls and like men's sins are,
    like the fruits of purgatory;
O the loquats Rosalinha
    plucks me from her backyard tree.

Dom Sebastião's Song
(Cape St Vincent)

> *He who goes to search for the bride in the noise of war*
> *dies without bride and without love, quite alone.'*
>   MIGUEL TORGA

> *Maybe, O shaman, your glance shall discern*
> *the ship in which the hidden one must return.*
>   ANTÓNIO SARDINHA

And how shall I come back from the dark
I who walked off the end of the world
crossed the sea's abyss to disembark
into the desert's impossible odds?

71

How then shall I come back from the dead
weapons burnished by the building sands
my supposed bones, rifled by wind, hid
in the gilded dune's reliquary?

How shall I take up my plundered pack
how shall I wake from a soldier's sleep
guitarra whose slack strings vultures pluck
to wake my lover who thinks me dead?

How arouse her who dreams me standing
beyond black water, both arms blessing
with, from my loins, a pontoon springing
sturdy bridge to carry her across?

How wake my lover who dreams me dead
gem in her casket, skull like amber
bleached and stretched on her ironing board
on her arm, walking, flesh round my feet?

How, like St Vincent, sail relics home
how harness ravens to this wreckage
how, in my lover's own time, return
wake the bereaved and waste their grieving?

My dreams of blood, the desert's ashes
sackcloth of sand and shame in battle
I'll renounce for a sailor's habit
and the dumb dunes for the prayerful swell.

My destination thyme and bugloss
stonechats' chime on the promontory
the rose of winds shall be my compass
westwards, a sunk sun boiling the sea.

Covered in darkness, swathed in sea-mist
unpierced by the navigator's gaze
by poet's eye or sacred lighthouse
I'll moor my wraith beneath the fortress.

Sleep on, my rival, landfall soft now
where the sea ends and the earth begins
I'll tiptoe home to my own pillow
surprise myself in my lover's arms.

KICKING SAWDUST

'When circus comes to town, the town dreams itself.'

to the memory of Philip Astley who in 1768
stood on horseback and traced the first modern ring

Ringmaster

Outside my canvas let the tempest roar!
At the still centre of this ring I prosper,
doff my top-hat, conjure my creatures' best.
Anarchy's ordered here. I'm self-possessed.
But on stark nights or stormy matinees
tent creaks, poles groan and guys grow mutinous;
fearful I'll lose my touch, loosen my grip,
I bind thongs to my wand and make a whip.

Fat Bearded Lady

I make a deep impression on the mud
of circus sites and on the gaping crowd
that shuffles through the turnstile to my booth
paying for generosity, for girth
and for the gall to show what they'd conceal
like secret sin beneath a cloak or shawl.
They hardly displace air. I laugh to see
them smirk and preen their slight normality.

Trapeze Artists

We swing like careless children, but sky-high:
work ourselves up, let ourselves go, and fly
or feint and seem to fall to make them gasp
and greedily gaze upwards as we grasp
pendulums that precisely intermesh
while, in the pit, drums roll and cymbals crash
swelling, as one, the public's appetite
like a fat spider in the safety net.

Lion-tamer

To spare the rod would be to spoil the lion.
I spoil him with red meat and comb his mane;
sometimes he smiles, or curls his snarling lip
and prowls about our cage with hackles up.
His rank breath gives me the sharp taste of truth
each time I stuff my face into his mouth.
I trust my luck, my lion, keep my head
and a tame marksman who can shoot him dead.

Knife-thrower

I have two aims. She has fine flesh, and trust
but blinks when I wink, Double-top? I lust.
Blindfolds, spread-eagle-spins, blades and close shaves.
We hold hands when we bow, then as she gives
me one coy kiss to please the audience
I smell her sweat, and wish she had more scents.
I love her faith, but long for her to feel
at closer range, warmer than naked steel.

Fire-eater

You laugh at fear, but duck when sawdust's thrown;
buckets of water douse the grinning clown.
We fly through air, or poise above an earth
that's hand in glove with gravity and death.
You gasp. We're in our element. Mine's fire.
I spew it, suck it, scald my mouth, singe hair;
no miracles, no Phoenix, just a spark
of old Prometheus or young Joan of Arc.

Juggler

The thought of keeping things up in the air
is simple and not easy. With a flair
for physics and pure physicality
I lend the practice blithe facility.
Elementary particles in orbit –
balls, flaming torches, furniture, clubs, fruit
have gravity; but my charmed hands exult,
just let things slip to make it difficult.

Strong Man

I am Sisyphus in leopard's clothing
with an uphill task: to conquer loathing,
grip the audience, snatch and jerk the weights.
My corset ruptures underneath my spots,
iron bars are scarfs, directories are torn
in twos, weaklings with kids applaud. Deep down,
they say, a hard-man is a gentle soul.
I'd lift and bend and rend them once for all.

Acrobats

A springboard and unparalleled physique
build little empires; with refined technique,
tough discipline, top-men and underdogs,
we leap and grip like frenzied mating frogs.
Despite the sweat, each human hieroglyph
looks cool, almost abstract: successive
triangles chalked up and wiped like Euclid's,
noble and useless as the pyramids.

Snake-woman

My constrictor's like a feather boa
that tickles me a little, nothing more.
The crowd's hugely amused, it's not quite nice
to see them so aroused. Snakes, chill as ice
but drier than men's skin, can stir or scare
them stiff. They leer and take me for a whore.
My serpents flatter me with their clear gaze;
I'm almost happy in a cool embrace.

Pickpocket

My victim volunteers and will submit
to the relief of braces, watch and wallet.
They applaud him, the scapegoat to be fleeced,
and me as each fresh crime is witnessed,
egging me on to take the liberty
of making public private property.
But as they exit they hold raincoats close,
outside the tent fear every kind of farce.

Midget

My stature makes me stand out in a crowd,
father and peer to every little kid.
In the Big Top I make my way, happy
like any showman when they clap me;
I whirl, a dwarfish dervish, on the mat
as well as any long-limbed acrobat
but wish I tumbled further when I fall,
wish I could stride unstilted, could walk tall.

Band Leader

I've my baton, the ringmaster his whip,
he rules the space but time is mine to keep:
I underscore each auguste clown's pratfall,
each tumbler's leap. Some will risk heart and soul
for the crowd's roar; my lads grudge lip and lung,
they'd play their socks off and remain unsung.
Crescendo. Kids' eyes are full of wonders,
fuller because my music fills their ears.

Human Cannonball

Though worn thin, keen to miss death by inches,
what artiste of my calibre flinches
at sliding down into the cannon's throat?
Held in its deafening hush I meditate.
I am attuned to the band's pulse, distant
but reassuring, till my assistant
springs me. Punched out into the world, I pause
safe in the net's embrace, and milk applause.

Clown

I am an artist playing to the mass,
the melancholy master on his arse.
To buckets, planks, each simple particle
I am the grand uncertain principal.
I grow refined, my props stay on the shelf,
against the world I pit merely myself
though one night, overweened with booze and pride,
I left the greasepaint off and children cried.

Sword-swallower

I am a dietician. Sharp flavours
tempt my trained palate and oesophagus.
It sickens folk to see that I don't retch
but gobble short swords, long swords with despatch,
taking each down to drum-rolls through clenched teeth.
People delight in my distaste for death,
my appetite. On their behalf I crave
the lethal blade and swallow it, and live.

Bareback Rider

I ride of course, but really I'm the box.
I take the tickets, and the bloody knocks
if bunce and stubs don't tally. Musn't whinge,
but I'm supposed to check it and then change
to risk my neck and whatnot, round and round.
Horses are nice. My feet don't touch the ground.
The strong-man's a wet fart. My man's a clown,
got our own trailer now. It's not much fun.

Tight-rope Walker

Old acrobat, I balance, belly full
of long-drawn battles with the sawdust's pull,
the flex and tug of arms jutting at air
like a drunk clutching at the furniture;
I win applause, not equilibrium,
exhausting pose and then the long climb down.
I want an act I know I can keep up,
the poise of a hanged man on his tight rope.

Stilt-walker

I condescend to give away balloons
then dwindle like a spire. Lofty buffoons
and elephants must lead the grand parade
to show off the dimensions of our trade:
your usual one-two-three, and less, and more,
down-at-heel freaks, athletes, fools on the floor.
Proud and precarious, we build big nights
while stray balloons cluster above the lights.

Elephant-girl

My spangled tail-coat's torn, my hat is flat,
my hair flies loose, the heel's come off one boot,
plinths crumble like anthills beneath the load
of antic elephants, who charge the crowd
plucking up poles like palms so sky falls down
as they dance quick-step, trumpeting in tune,
grey rocks or clouds that crush me like a worm.
Before we hit the road I get this dream.

Ringmaster

I have bowed out, music and lights have died,
we strike the ring and watch our world subside
with one languorous sigh. The king-pole's felled.
There is no wake, just work. I too, toppled
from king to jack, king-pin to handy-man,
hustler and clerk who pays the rent and then
moves on to hire things, turns and pastures new,
leaving a ring of bleached grass to the dew.

* * *

Luminous Lover

(Ottawa 1922)

Luminous lover
I kissed her fine
and I've kissed her now
for the very last time

Oh I loved the lips
of my painter girl
as she sucked her brush
to a pointed curl

I'd stack and sweat
deep in the store
jealous of her painting
on the factory floor

Clocks and watches
coming down the line
always said she painted
to pass the time

Painted all the numbers
from twelve to one
big hands and little hands
luminous green

And I loved the lips
of my painter girl
as she sucked her brush
to a pointed curl

Through the Depression
we earned good pay
had a real high time
my lover and I

On early turn late turn
turning all the while
more than a hand's turn
at Radium Dials

Now I turn in my bed
in the lonely night
staring out the time
the time's so bright

Dream how the girls
made up for a laugh
with luminous eyebrows
lipstick and teeth

And I loved the lips
of my painter girl
as she sucked her brush
to a pointed curl

So open wide
say Ah! if you can
swell up your cheeks
put out your tongue

Too many sick ones
too many dead
quinsy or diptheria
the doctors said

They paid off the doctors
paid attorneys too
we couldn't prove nothing
nothing we could do

Now the factory's gone
bright times have passed
it's a parking lot
where the geiger ticks fast

Oh I loved the lips
of my painter girl
as she sucked her brush
to a pointed curl

My luminous lover
I kissed her fine
and I've kissed her now
for the very last time

When Waves Give Up Their Dead

(Royal Adelaide, Chesil Bank, 25 November 1872)

> *When the sea gives up her dead it will be a host uncountable who will crowd the steep sides of the amphitheatre of Deadman's Bay.*
> FREDERICK TREVES

And when the waves give up their dead
I'll dance on the grinding shore
to watch the Royal Adelaide
and hear the pebbles roar

She tried to beat out of the bay
all that afternoon befogged
and fighting a sou'westerly
until her anchors dragged

So here's a landfall everyone
here's a gale to warp the stars
all on the London-Sydney run
poor emigrants and tars

Soon after dark it was she struck
broadside on the pebble ridge
2,000-ton clipper-built barque
hard by the Ferry Bridge

Tar barrels, torches, flares were lit
ghostly hills of water fell
upon a ship that soon must split
it was a glimpse of hell

Sailors with lanterns ran on deck
swung like dolls against a hull
that shuddered, lurched and snuffed their spark
flesh and stones, bone and skull

A force that nothing could outrun
took the ship up in its fists
cracked ribs, snapped spars and one by one
snipped off her masts

We gathered on the Chesil Bank
saw her rigging churned like wrack
and sensed her anguish as she sank
and felt her break her back

Victims screamed but no one heard
as spume burst in the vessel's shell
and shook the stones on which we stood
it was a snatch of hell

When flotsam spirits bumped ashore
kegs were broached to toast her crew
each spilt long rations down his maw
and down each others' too

So here's a windfall, here's a wake
here's a gale to steal your breath
and with a life-long thirst to slake
we drank ourselves to death

At dawn the storm-clouds went aground
gulls croaked and curious dogs
nuzzled the sexless ageless drowned
and revellers cold as logs

Their ship came home and so did mine
all foundered in that gale
when some of us sank too much brine
some too much alcohol

I'll swill rum yet at Ferry Bridge
by the ghostly Adelaide
and dance along the rattling ridge
when waves give up their dead

Wormwood

This is a martial herb, and is governed by Mars.
CULPEPER

And the third angel sounded, and there fell a great star from heaven,
burning as it were a lamp…And the name of the star is called
wormwood: and the third part of the waters became wormwood;
and many men died of the waters, because they were made bitter.
REVELATION 8, 10 & 11

This plant belongs to Mars.
It grows on the banks of the Dnieper.
In low potency it cures
nervous tremors, deliriums,
hallucinations, terrors
and poisoning by mushrooms.
Its leaves are grey and downy
and it is bitter.

It blooms in June and July
on waste land in dry regions
and thrives on the banks of the Dnieper.
As *absinthe* it engenders
nervous tremors, deliriums,
hallucinations, terrors,
in excess. In moderation
it is a tonic.

It sends Soviet citizens
back to their bibles,
communists and christians
suffering tremors and terrors,
the bitter text: in Ukrainian
'wormwood' is *chernobyl*.
Chernobyl on the banks of the Dnieper.
This plant belongs to Mars.

The New Water Music

The sun tumbles the shadows of things headlong,
wrings infra-red from boles and jagged reed-beds.
Duck, unreflecting, stand on the lake's skin
or touch down skittering and more ungainly
than the fifth generation of computers.

Sky-striding heron damps its neck's sine-wave.
The ice aches for catastrophe. My pratfalls prompt
geese to akimbo silent-movie rushes
at take-off. I, too, uncertain and more gauche
than the fifth generation of computers

with my tragic sense. My carelessly-flung stones
strike vacant ice and synthesise a music
of pure whiplashes – *faz-zang, faz-zong, faz-zung* –
worth more than these poor ears, this air, that sun,
worthy of chaos and equilibrium.

Seeing Her Across

Each weekday morning in term-time
   I walk to the main road,
my stick under my arm and warmth
   of my child's hand in mine.

She step-steps for each stride I make,
   she stops me at the kerb;
we hear the cars, she looks both ways,
   squeezes my hand and runs.

Those who can see will understand
   each day holds its small loss.
I turn, my stick tap-taps back home
   from seeing her across.

No Before or After

To this, there's no before or after.
It stands between delirium and
delirium, hole in a frosted pane,
a window out of time. And not a dream.

I see, close up, above the picture rail,
fine cracks and paper puckered where walls
meet ceiling at the corner of my room.
No nightmare this. Cracks do not open.

I seem to turn and look down on my bed
whose rumpled covers are like ripples
cast into relief by window-shine,
the curtains slightly swaying, and frozen.

It's no surprise it's my face on the pillow;
my mother bends and blots it out, bathing
my brow, the doctor times my pulse, his hair
is thinning, reads the thermometer

he has just taken from between my lips,
lays my arm down and shakes his head. I
can feel none of this. I see it all.
I can see care, so clearly. Then I fall.

Right of Passage

(Parkstone)

I liked the street I played in
as a kid, but for one house
that lurked behind its trees,
peered over unpruned shrubs
and overgrown weed beds:
I grew to love that one.

I grew to love my fears
of the dark lives that moved
in there; the black-haired witch
with huge breasts swinging deep
inside a thinning vest
over man's belt and trousers.

I only saw her when she swept
the quilt of dead leaves off her step
while a great ogre at the window,
in motley stains and buttons,
fag in mouth, shouted 'Come in
you hag,' shouted and wept.

Once a slow motion gin bottle
exploded under me and plucked
the spokes as I biked past,
'Get off my pavement, bastard!'
No blood or punctures proved
me invulnerable.

Still, I was nervous when he loomed
in suit and hat and buttonhole
outside the barber's where I'd propped
my guy. He dropped me sixpence
'for Guy fucking Fawkes'. I knew
then that my love was doomed.

On his way home from a long sup
he smiled. I liked my street now
without fear or risk of love.
He slipped me half-a-crown,
'And may you blow the whole
of bloody Parkstone up.'

This Is Our House

Door's smaller than the windows and shut tight,
roof swells like sea, chimney's a tall cigar,
path twists like smoke between the starry flowers.
Beside the house a woman stands up straight,
her yellow hair would fill the whole top floor.
This is our house, I done it just for you.

People won't fit inside, the child knows that.
Ground floor is clenched around a chuckling fire,
bedrooms billow with dreams, attic is fat
with dark that won't leak from the chimney-pot,
the child knows that. She'll try, her with the hair,
to get back in and clean it through and through.

Granny's Gloves
(Digitalis alba)

The blackest thing about the snow fox
is its spoor, a devious dream
stalking the dense waste of the cortex

There, at the parting of grandmother's hair
through her thin scalp, I thought I saw
her fine face purpled and heart snared

Then 'Digitalis!' attack after attack
restored her pallor and damped fibrillations
each time but one the foxglove brought her back

These seeds will quicken, and slow grief
with quilted green, octaves of fingers
all her Edwardian summers' gloves

Much later, I can see her head of hair
watching the white globe of the moon
on TV, and the footprints there

'That's the moon, granny, men in space'
and she, 'Where are they really?'
Her pityingly indulgent gaze

It is an old tune their hearts strum
upon a figment of our gravity
up where the hare sleeps in its form

But she sees some north-polar comic turn
or flour-mill robots, not that lunar light
in which no foxgloves wax or wane

And I am seeing sutures, snow-fox track
stroking the white hair that I love
sensing the wild one double back, and back

Where starry flowers flank lanes too deep
for gigs to pass unscathed, she saw
thorn hedge-banks snatching at black crêpe

I see the purples nodding in her wake
and in the autumn I will plant capsules
of green, white heat for summer's sake

Struck

Not liking women much, I knew I'd stick
at home, upright and strong to run the farm
thinking that as you aged, dad, you'd retire
from field and yard back to the kitchen range
where mother and the kettle sang all day.
Her dead, I thought you'd tidy, wash and cook
while I made money selling milk and beef.
That's how it was before the lightning struck.

I stick at home. Outside I lean and look
at the horizon just one field away;
what land we haven't sold you hedge and ditch,
I stack the sticks or creosote the shed.
Inside all's shine, soap, disinfectant.
We make do on the Pension and the Sick
plus wily deals you do on market day,
stay proud despite the fact that lightning struck.

Twisted and crochety, I curse the muck
your boots bring in; shriek that your dinner's cold;
all weathers, air my washing at the stove;
send you, all weathers, out to smoke your pipe.

I'm mother here, since one bolt felled the cow
I milked, corkscrewed my spine and seared my back.
You scrub hands twice a day and dress the wound
that's not stopped weeping since the lightning struck.

Lane's End

The farm gate rattles,
mostly it's the wind.
One track into the world
the distance like a wall
the space a prison, acres
whose harvests come and come
and come to mock me here.
Him, his skin like earth
trespassing in my bathroom.
His granaries, for all he sucks
from bottles, richly swelling
and his man, young man
who has a life
because he lives elsewhere.
Their arms rest on my table
their silences agree
and exile me again.

I could break something
silence, teapot, vows.
I talk day long
calling myself to order
order against the tide
of straw and mud and shit
and my dark blood.
I twitch the sheets tight
on our mattresses.
I twit him and I tempt
kind words from his young man.
Something must disagree.
Across the fields the chapel
the hay-bed in the barn
the bottle by my pillow
that does not swill like his
but rattles, rattles.

Anosmia

No nose for anything now.
He mourns the singular smell of fear
the plural scents of love. Subtle
losses grieve him, not bland flowers.

He eats, but misses the flavours,
piles sugar in his cup, salt
on his plate. He has a tongue for
memories, sourness and sweetness.

He tastes sweet rain upon cut grass
and the sea, he loves the sea,
the tides in the wind. Unsubtle
like sexual juice, like hot tears.

The Pangs of Words

Years on I feel again, again the shock
of your slow dying and your death –
if the possessive adjective applies.
Yours became ours. All your friends mourned.
I grieved for you but not, I think, enough.

Heart-sickness that ambushes me today
is not old ravening grief
but love which your death and my life betrayed;
love which we had and would not hold
because you had a man and I a wife.

It was denial but not punishment.
Which hurts most, past tense or passive
mood? For far too long I've framed the words
my mouth last printed on your skin.
Now I mourn me you loved, and you in health.

I'll celebrate you whole to cure myself:
your pressure, colour, smell. My love
– if the possessive adjective applies –
you knew the pangs of words; that grief
does not quite rhyme with death, nor love with life.

Invisible Ink

Here are the love letters I've not written.
Bring your face close and breathe
the slight perfume imbuing each unsent page,
something of soil, rain, something of flowers.
Watch the snow sheet. Writing unravels
like wire that runs away into the wood
and over the hill. See telegraph poles
sprout roots and branches, the trees whispering.

See lightnings flare along the horizon
and ink in all the nerve-ends of the skin.
Close your eyes, listen, the wires run deep
down beyond the skyline, poles tall, nerves taut,
branches and roots, roots and branches like nets
snaring the rocks, our clouds. Searching. Leafing.
Open your eyes, see how the floor is filling
with all the love letters I've not written.

Room Enough

Perhaps this room begins
as a cupboard where toys
fall over themselves to
spill into light of play
or huddle on the night's
shadowy floor, yearning
to be tidied away.

Perhaps it is a closet
sparse with sacred creatures
ebony wand, gold ring
snakeskin and hollow bone
alert for their fleshing,
too awful to open
without lips frame their spell.

Or a room with a bed
where long lithe bodies meet
where hungry mouths swap tongues
where words are swallowed down
distilled to their juices
erotic essences
while the minds go hunting.

Perhaps it detaches
itself from the kitchen
the study, the garden.
Perhaps the room floats free
and we fleshy spirits
fumble for the pass-key
to cupboard, closet, vault.

Our hands land on the latch
offer each the penthouse
the stable-suite, the barn
in which tamed wild things rut
for our domestication
where deft spiders weave and
bats wing of their own will.

Now we have found a room
in the wind between rains
between wood and midden
under the holly bush
under the light we lie
naked with our clothes on
or off, our hair falling.

Here we caress our pelts
here words enter our ears
here eyes flame clear, flesh weeps
pursed and pierced, soft as felt
hilt hard against bone-shield
whole skins incandescent
sun shafts, here in this room.

Now it chooses its walls
as the mind the brain-pan
as the body its bones
as whole meets whole and grows
so that it terrifies
whatever's left outside
embraces all we know.

It is complete, but keeps
asking for completeness.
The wind kicks the door in
curtains flail like ghost flags
flushing the room of us
I quail, you moan but it's
your cheek my tears dry on.

In the morning we leave
the room empty, the world
larger for us, but small.
Each re-enters thinking
the other is still there.
Each, alarmed, has to love
the world where we still are.

This not the recipe
for ruin, monument
to love. This not a shell
but dome split open for
the dance of little deaths
that with the elements
storms, storms the open door.

Reprieve

Though wanting me, you granted a reprieve
and ran for sweet life, swearing that you'd stay:
you loved so dearly that you had to leave.

You wore my heart for months upon your sleeve
but in your marrow sensed an old dismay.
Though wanting me you granted a reprieve

I hadn't asked, for how should I conceive
of such desire wishing itself away?
You loved, so dearly that you had to leave

me sick and angry that you could deceive,
committing yourself only to betray,
though wanting, me. You granted a reprieve

from your dark dreams, intricate and naive,
which tangled love with death and night with day;
you loved so dearly that you had to leave.

You hated to destroy or undeceive
yourself and me, but chose to end the play:
though wanting me you granted a reprieve,
you loved so dearly that you had to leave.

POEMS OF Z

*– in memory of my father who knew how to talk
and of my mother who knew how to sing*

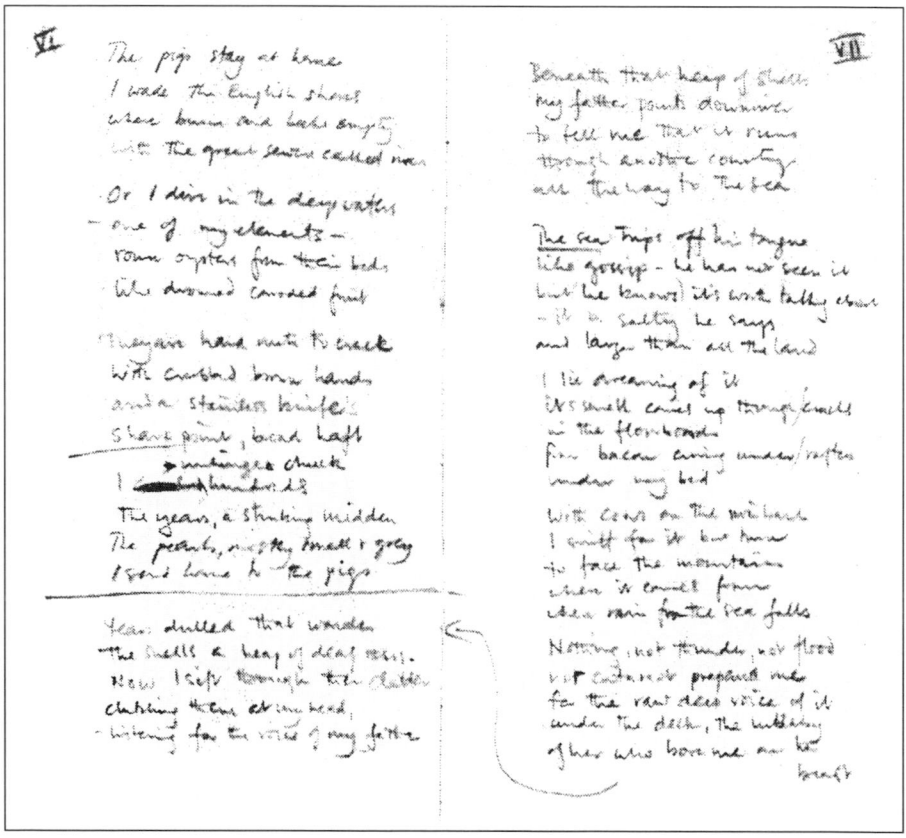

Pages from Z's notebook

PREFACE

It will be clear why it is difficult for me to disclose how these poems came into my possession. Their unexpectedness and their unexpected power, that made such an impact on me, are the important things about them. In any case, I have nothing illuminating to say about their background, for all my knowledge of it comes from them. All I have is a small, rather dog-eared notebook of forty unlined pages, each with a poem pencilled upon it in English. The dedication and the quotations from Lear and Jonson are scribbled inside the front cover. At the head of the first page is written *Poems of Z*.

In passing Z's notebook to the publisher I have become involved in preparing the poems for the press. When he made revisions Z's usual practice was, it seems, to erase the original – 'pencil stitched/ and smudged across a grubby page' – but where he has not done this I have taken the two readings as alternatives, and have chosen the one I judged the better. I have also made a small handful of amendments to Z's sparse punctuation, for the sake of clarity or consistency.

Z seems to have been engaged in intelligence activities in the UK for a number of years. The poems are certainly about that, but I think it unlikely that our counter-espionage service will glean much from these pages. The poet – for this is what, in a crisis of self-examination, Z became – is not concerned with 'Names and Places/Technical Detail, Plans/Political Praxis, Miscellaneous'; he asks 'What does the heart know', and writes of his own tenderness and violence, duplicity and openness, his faithlessness and spiritual hunger. From his world within our world, employing our language, he casts a cool eye on England,' 'the England I love'. He speaks movingly of the world of his childhood; the spy remembers his father and writes:

> ... all the seasons
> gone for which he, his weathered face
> upturned, gathered intelligence

Here we have an extraordinary view of an extraordinary poetic development. The start must have been tentative, but once assured of what he was about I feel sure that Z wrote the poems as they stand in the notebook, one after another, each dependent on the one before, each qualified by the next. They demonstrate a sharpening of vision and a hardening of intention probably unsuspected at the outset. The naivety of the enterprise was to Z, I think, an essential element of it. Its success was perhaps as much of a surprise to him as it is to us. He felt it was not attainable in his own language. That Z should write so well in English is surely remarkable, but it is also crucial to his purpose:

101

            I need decode the words
            I do it in English
            I adopt that tongue

Towards the end he anticipates returning home and recalls M***
(an informant?) who returned 'from the fascists' hands' with his
tongue cut out:

            muscles at his tongue's
            root fought with the air
            in his open mouth

            a crock at the end
            of an arc of blood.
            We cried out for him

Z has left us forty poems.

PAUL HYLAND

Thou whoreson zed! thou
unnecessary letter!
— LEAR

Z is a letter often heard
amongst us, but seldome seene.
— JONSON

I

This is sudden
this to be a poet

A need my comrades
would scoff at
if they knew, scoff
in our own tongue –

You an agent
from a thriller's cover
you a blank face
under a black hat

You a poet – I say it
too in my own tongue

I need decode the words
I do it in English
I adopt that tongue
it moves differently
in my mouth, it swells

If across these pages
it speaks I will hand them
to my friend the professor
at S***, he will translate
back into my own tongue

That will not be sudden
that handing over
this notebook when it is full

II

This is like taking off clothes
heavy coats one at a time
each one less burden
the weight of keeping warm
gone in a room with oil-light
and water breathing in iron

That's what it's like shedding
clothes, hardware, braces,
trousers and at the end
no shame. No shame

In a room with oil-light
lying in elbow-warm water
the grown flesh fallen away
bathing in the iron bath
supported by my mother's arm
her free hand rinsing my limbs

She sings to me in my own tongue
songs I will forget in London
I pitch my gurgles back to her
my poems she can't understand

III

You see there is nothing
naive and sentimental as
a grown man with soft hands
and a calloused heart
starting out as poet

The idea of it anyway.
From my rented table
through the spacious grid
of sash windows I keep
watch on Georgian London

As I once spied from a pane
set into thick thatch
on my father in the yard
the pigs rooting, my sisters
walking out in the wood

when I should have been sleeping.
Opposite, the porticoes in line
the columns and pediments
all at once I am astonished
at the weight of masonry

I walk in and out of every day

IV

In the streets of language
I need no maps any more.
If I were to try words of love
my tongue would taste
of their dust and litter

Intimacy that is paid for –
after sleepless nights sometimes
street signs are foreign flags
pinned to great architecture
roads veer off at wrong angles

I am a beast turned drab
driven in from the far country
to scavenge in dustbins
and basement entries
tainted by offal and old bones

My lack of condition
my dullness is protective
colouration for mission
the noblest drive of my kind
to survive, depraved appetite

This pencil and paper
my belting bark that should
fly meadows and pierce woods
pitched off monstrous buildings
in the streets of language

V

As a boy I was one
learning to be more

One with the pigs in their pen
far inland chucking them acorns
from a holed bucket,
the sea a dream of passion

One with my sisters' boys
little man among little men
One with my aunt in town
in my white stiff things

One for my first communion
One for the party, party-man
In London now I am Legion
for we are many

I would invite my pigs here
for my first communion –
they would rush outwards
in all directions

And every English shore
they dashed themselves over
trotters gashing own throats
would wash with their gore

I would be one
I have learned to be more

VI

The pigs stay at home
I wade the English shores
where burns and becks empty
with great sewers called rivers

Or I dive in the deep waters
– one of my elements –
rouse oysters from their beds
like drowned corroded fruit

They are hard nuts to crack
with crabbed brown hands
and a stainless knife's
sharp point, broad haft

I unhinge and chuck hundreds
the years, a stinking midden
the pearls, mostly small and grey
I send home to the pigs

VII

Beneath that heap of shells
my father points downriver
to tell me that it runs
through another country
all the way to the sea

The sea trips off his tongue
like gossip – he has not seen it
but knows it's worth talking about
– it is salty he says
and larger than all the land

I lie dreaming of it
its smell comes up through
cracks in the floorboards
from bacon curing under
rafters under my bed

With cows on the riverbank
I sniff for it but turn
to face the mountains
where it comes from
where rain from the sea falls

Nothing, not thunder, not flood
nor cataract prepared me
for the raw deep voice of it
under the deck, the lullaby
of her who bore me on her breast

Years dulled that wonder
the shells a heap of deaf ears.
Now I sift through their clatter
clutching them at my head
listening for the voice of my father

VIII

I creep nearer and nearer
– my sisters hide their faces
even safe inside the house –
the nuzzled ground slavers
and sucks at my shoes

I creep close to my father
and his friend G***
and the pale pig standing
bound between them
father shaving its throat

A quick sliced stab and blood
– though I know it trickled
I see it spurt in an arc
a thick monotonous rainbow
caught in a crock

The arc of the pig's scream
stopped in my ears –
ten minutes before silence
trotters trying to flail
blond eyelashes still

Only when the blood stops
at last I start to cry
a complicated wailing
father reproves with his glare
to my sisters' scorn I creep away

IX

That was the first time
I approached slow death
under a waxing moon

Father's apprentice, I know
the pig's swan-song well
never two the same

I know it well, I feel it
coming from the throat
the beast's strain in my hands

My hands shake as I write
I can't translate, in English
I cannot make you hear it

X

My mother's stitchery
by oil-light, bright needle
pricking linen with petals
taut as a tambourine
beneath tight black eyes

Come quick, my father calls
come do something useful.
She anchors the skein
who never did anything
not useful, but this

They kneel down together
in the sty by oil-light
the feverish sow between them
a small sister, brown hands
travelling her white lard

Your mother was beautiful
father tells me one day.
It is a strange saying.
His eyes that have known more
than mine seem to see less

That fine work by oil-light
he tells her, wrinkles your eyes
but occasions for it
don't stop, nor she, save to suck
new silk for the needle's eye

All her care is dispersed
now, given or gone away
under some several roofs
my sisters and I
all her useless stitchery

XI

I have a piece here in London
made of stitches I cannot name
in English, let alone my tongue

A blue bird perched on a green branch
among red blooms but faded, old
linen yellowed at every fold

It is like my heart, packed, unpacked
furled and unfurled in foreign rooms
hid in the luggage of my limbs

On my table in this blank book
I trace the profile of that heart
with pencil, rubber and no art

In this ageing and English light
it's hard to read, too dark at times
to write, seeing so little rhymes

Or too much chimes unjustly –
were they all silken lies she told
that ate now mellowed and grown old

This one, hung in my tall white room
stretched again, gilt-framed and fading
dimmed by the light I see it in

The light I work by, pencil stitched
and smudged across a grubby page
dazzles my eyes with the heart's rage

XII

And each plough-time the heavy horse
leans at unbroken ground, the share
burnished of rust at the first turn
first furrow, the year's paradigm

The soil's breath breaks intact from it
and birds hang on its lips, I pass
en route for school and my return
sees father's warp stretched hedge to hedge

I learn my letters, figures too
he broadcasts over harrowed land
I weave between the feint ruled lines
his testament, my exercise

At home my head buried in books
The first cuckoo! my father calls
Can you hear it? Of course I can
I do not know why I say no

I am bored with the grand routine
that feeds me, the man who works it.
My hunger is for print; his, corn
in stitch, weather's embroidery

His labour is all harvested
sewing unpicked, all the seasons
gone for which he, his weathered face
upturned, gathered intelligence

XIII

There is one place I know
where the street smells right
in Soho, a café where I go
sometimes, where they sell
the right sort of bread

and where they speak my tongue
among themselves. I listen
with the other foreigners
the English men, I sink
my teeth in the bread

and roll it on my tongue
how sourdough sweetens!
and swallow it hard

XIV

The priest throws back his head
under the uptilted chalice

Under the black of his beard
his supple throat pumps

As if he emptied the dome
of the psalms lapping its brim

And on my tongue dissolution
of wafer and high seriousness

The creed's sumptuous chant
strangely bland but indigestible

Because I think I could not give
all my juices to it; flatus

In the bowel lent a pained smile
to the practice of holiness

To him whose racked form rode the tree
into whose death I could not donate

Suffering so framed with pomp
but I see now in retrospect

Not wholly corrupt, a memory
a drinking to certain hope

The priest's voluptuous throat
throbbing with joyous guffaws

Celebrating a death and again
roaring at the death of death

XV

Then I was consecrated
to correct economics
I was a bright pupil

Now with a dull eye
I look out from London
across foothills of brick

Domes and spires diminished
douched by a cataract
of glass, architect's vision

I had it, I saw man
pinned on the drawing-board
in plan and elevation

My tall head built of panes
tears of glass sizzled
on the dome of my heart

Theoretical pity
for the man I had seen
not for me, not for me

I had not yet learned that.
I was a bright pupil.
Now with a dull eye

I creep through porticoes
pitiful, not a cubit
added to my stature

XVI

(Is it worth it
this dredging up
memories of

the future that
is long gone and
that never was?

Worth anything
to think of the
position to

which ambition
raised me, me and
all of mankind

it imagined?
Since I have been
put in my place

probably it
is worthless but
it is costly)

XVII

I was a saint, for love
of country I left it –
frontiers as are well known
are imaginary
and bloody – my ideals
in the safe custody
of trustworthy comrades

Like a child who's lent
toys to fickle friends
I fear to return

What of my toys amongst
the pieces they picked up
the imaginary
and ransacked nursery
pieced together again
piecemeal, beloved country
ramshackle in my head

I want to visit
but I hesitate
to go back, for good

XVIII

The ship I came on
passport to mission
iron link with home
(the farewell handprint
of my dead father
on its starboard rail)
the subtle groundswell
sickness at parting
embarking upon
something

       When I heard
(from fellow-exiles
I can't call comrades)
that the vessel C***
survivor of war
by accident, had
long been broken up
steep deck, raucous plates
all scrap, in a gust
old salt stung my eyes

XIX

My sentimentality appals me
then consoles; emotions still, but sudden
I butter-fingered drop them and mis-feel

I was a hard nut in my prime to crack
a mind and body bedded snugly in
well knitted joints, nothing rotten or loose

But then a place grew softly where they met
back of the throat, perhaps, above the heart
grew large and liquid, a soft centre, sac

Whose juice digests my thick skin from within
and now I think my insides are all slops
contained tears pent up in a fragile shell

I am a hard man before breaking out
I shall, if I hole myself, leak away.
I am appalled, to hatch now is to die

XX

I do not listen much
to fellow-exiles' tales
of home, they must believe
they are better off here
since they cannot return

I do not listen much
because I can, but one
such bitter recital
nestles deep in my ear
like a worm, a tale of

imaginative torture –
a troublesome priest penned
in B*** prison, at length
exhorted by a spike
red hot steel up his arse

on his knees to say mass
over shit and piss
though ordure and urine
were the words the man used
who told the tale, shaking

I don't know if I should
take his words for gospel
his imagination
or my lack of it, fact
it is best to forget

Facts are made up. To know
from far, to remember
is to daydream. Bread. Shit.
To see straight in close-up
an imaginative act

XXI

I have nothing to say in return
missionary without a gospel

lamp hid under a bushel
me in this airless room!

you think I've escaped to this
from the pig-pen, my trampled country

or am expatriate on greener grass
mixing my hopes and fears with yours

my conversation is a charade
I watch from under word-cover

when I re-enter my homeland
I shall shout hopes out loud

I'm no exile banished from my soil
exile is my mission

patriot, servant, soon I shall return
till then this pencil is blunted

re-sharpened, otherwise never share
my fears with anyone, anywhere

XXII

My parents' business
always was well-known
in the next village
before ours because
our clear-eyed neighbour
silent Mother K***

had a garrulous
sister living there
to whom each Sunday
she'd carefully walk
with white eggs and take
brandy in return

retracing her steps
with a happily
empty basket just
as her darling hens
were cackling over
their darling white eggs

XXIII

Prayer was often difficult
the confessional was an easy route
to God's ear – it was his eye
I feared glinting through lattice-work

The presumptive photo of me
was taken before my first communion
crisp and black and white – his eye
an open shutter between prayers

snapping at each new secret sin
a series of mug-shots falling away
from the primal image – I
tried to surprise myself in mirrors

to find out if anything showed
the complexion of my soul seeping through
an aperture – that his eye
would scan, find wanting and write down

I could not find words for my sins
I repented of faith in forgiveness
penance mere punishment – I
feared passing of notes and whispering

XXIV

The hospital
– me a boy
in a men's ward –
I love the whole
the real world

Stethoscopes read
universal tremors
world of diagnoses
screens dragged around
trivial atrocities

and unlikely cures
starched sheets and
disinfectant
covering up
for corruption

I love it all
the noise of life
silence of death
orchestrated
out of control

Doctors bending over
listening with
their instruments
their smiles and
their knowledge

or what is not worse ignorance
ignorance
I love it all
a museum
of living sicknesses

as I love England

XXV

In the England I love
I am visitor
I am listener
and collector

I step out stooping
from the sick-room
the confessional
and the hen-coop

With my stethoscope
my white coat
and a notebook
full of symptoms

With my micro-camera
under my cassock
with white eggs
cradled in my smock

XXVI

When the air though cold
hung heavily in the trees
I heard a pig's scream
and looked out – an arena
at the forest's edge
where a desperate dog-wolf
chased one of our young

A piglet runs like a cat
ears flat, stops so fast
with all its trotters dug in
grinning in its fear
that the grey beast overruns
and snarling turns back
on the pale scampering thing

Then it seems success
turns the pig's head from terror
to playfulness till
its squealing is with laughter
and the dog-wolf too
relaxes despite hunger
fangs sure then of lard

Whether or not I dreamt this
or saw in the flesh
circus at the forest's edge
when the air though cold
hung heavily in the trees
I heard the pig's scream
bubble softly and turn red

XXVII

What I am does not add up
then I think
that always there's a big bomb
in the air

Plane circling above England
on alert
ready to head east before
you can blink

All is in order up there
precision
double-checked triple-fail-safe
on target

Above smiling diplomats
governments
and people making mistakes
making love

I think of just one of them
just one crew
made one through harsh discipline
conditioned

Made interrogation-proof
by torture
dependable tools put through
my paces

I am of their brotherhood
I encode
the world's everyday chaos
my cover

When I wonder what I am
I think of
this life of ours, men plus bombs
I add up

XXVIII

I am not Samson
pillars and porticoes
do not give way
at my weight
I am not blind

I watch the faces
listen to gossip
corridors and closets
whispers of free speech
this democracy

A house divided
against itself
– eyes already
clogged with coin –
does not need Samson

XXIX

In my country
we look into each other's eyes
freedom has been won

The victors have given it to us
– if freedom is everything
that is what we owe them

When a man dies his son
eats the bacon that cures
under the dead man's rafters

The chandelier's contagion inherited
by blood: the victors' heirs
preserve our freedom, salt it down

We are hungry
the flesh of our house whole
but divided in spirit

We look into each other's eyes
first one way and then another
first one way and then another

XXX

I am a puppet
on very long strings

length gives a certain
elasticity

Or

I am a part of
a ventriloquist's act

I sit very still
and keep my mouth shut

I am a dummy
on the knee of a

cadaver

XXXI

My face a professional dissident
I stretch to fit the mask

My heart a muscle-knot
can't afford feeling
acts by the method
– empathy disallowed-
objective performance
happy when the audience
turns away, coughs behind its hand

My head a cabinet
of files each labelled
Faces, Names and Places
Technical Detail, Plans
Political Praxis, Miscellaneous
classified according to
priority and secrecy

Watch, listen to the audience
collate
designate
transmit
adrenalin
instinct
the head gathers intelligence

The face knows nothing
the heart knows something else

XXXII

What does the heart know
it is not certain

the heart is in exile
and not from its soil

Voltaire's tragic figure
the faithless priest

the heart thought it escaped
God and his trappings

left home for the night
like my grown sisters

drowning the pigs' musk
with toilet water

carrying their smart shoes
as far as the road

lodging boots in the hedge
against their return

the heart has grown up twice
faithless atheist

Materialism & History
are not enough

I want more I want more
the hungry heart

I know about hunger
when there is no food

but no, not when there is
no such thing as food

XXXIII

Lately, perhaps because I soon shall cross it
for the last time, I have been tripping
to the sea

And what seems like a mote troubles my eye
a man's head floating far out, fighting
with the sea

Imaginary and bloody frontier –
stones, fine red fronds like hands' veins
in the sea

Unaccounted-for corpuscles per cubic metre
and only great mammals warming the dilute blood
of the sea

I pick up soft pebbles of chalk, sculpture
burrowed-in, bored-through, dense with the dead
of the sea

My size is embarrassing suddenly, my pride –
what do I know of the creaturely galaxies
in the sea

And what of the man I imagine
far out, trampled in the waves' charge, drowning
in the sea.

I know nothing, I turn back to the low cliffs
their dirty-red and grey houses blindly looking
out to sea

And I think I throw my shoes off and dive in
a good socialist or a bourgeois hero
by the sea

My victim does not appreciate the difference
I buoy him up, he cries Save me, save me
from the sea

XXXIV

Soon I shall board a plane
and fly from one language
to another. It will
take a part of a day

I shall fly from English
even from these poems
back to my tongue. I still
think of it in that way

All my intelligence
flew that route under wraps
and waits for me. There I'll
be day by day by day

Transmitted, translated
back in time to the tongue
I was taught in. The thrill
of seeing, then, one way

Before that, older games
of dreams and sense and faith
long forgotten. My skill
with each word a new toy

I'll think of my poems
this intelligence in
my other tongue. I will
not be a sad old boy

XXXV

I am flying to my homeland
I will not be a sad old boy

My father is long dead
I will not be a sad old boy

My mother is dead also
I will not be a sad old boy

My sisters are still alive
I will not be a sad old boy

My wife is not any more
I will not be a sad old boy

My work is over and done with
I will not be a sad old boy

My time is up it is too late
I will not be a sad old boy

My time is my own
I will not be a sad old boy

What time?
I will not be a sad old boy

I've been saying it over and over
like a charm, a strong charm
repeated under a waxing moon
or litany, endless litany
chanted to ward off the devil
or a prayer, a heart-felt prayer
a begging letter

XXXVI

(Fortunately from
an objective viewpoint
I am unimportant

I serve the state
a people's monk
an eye on a stalk

my feelings and my fate
the last things
I should think about

I look out for the rest
why worry them
with my hope and guilt

I am unimportant
it takes so many me's
to make a mass)

XXXVII

I have not mentioned it yet
– a man in my position
has to be discreet with women –
but since I left my wife behind
a succession of at best
brief happinesses has dogged me

I think of my mother and father.
My eyes have known more than theirs
but seem to see less. I do not
wonder at my heaviness.
Eyes' saturated humours
precipitate a callus on the nerve

that only tears can solve.
However tenderly it was done
it has all been snatched and stashed
in the memory. Nothing was made.
Now I want to make it up
with somebody, in my tongue, at home

XXXVIII

What shall I say now
with this English tongue
cut out of my head

(M*** whom we thought lost
came back from the dead
from the fascists' hands

He had lost his tongue.
They had translated
him into a fool

forgetting how well
fools are listened to,
his eloquent hands

muscles at his tongue's
root fought with the air
in his open mouth

a crock at the end
of an arc of blood.
We cried out for him)

I have not suffered
not really, I am
it seems in one piece

and if we're careful
my friend, professor
at S***, will translate

all this, this false start
back into my tongue.
I may find my tongue

XXXIX

During the war –
men at men's throats
– how we trusted
our poor neighbours
we thought we knew
who our friends were

So I'll propose
a special vote
of thanks to friends
here in England
for trusting me –
here's to neighbours!

Do not disturb
was my watchword-
if he'll forgive
a spy's foibles
I'll forgive the
drunkard next door

Leave him in peace

XL

On leaving shall I pronounce
as retiring episkopos
benediction on my diocese?

Shall I quote Jesus, My peace
I leave with you? I would not bequeath
my whatever it is to a dog

In peace is passive enough,
your choice. Peace does not belong to me
I am going home to look for it

Shall I quote the prodigal,
Father I have sinned? I cannot tell
if I'm moving to or from the pig-pen

Because I'm taking myself with me
I'm taking myself to the banquet
I shall say grace

*   *   *

Sharp and Sweet

How sweet and sharp they tasted, those
   apples we scrumped
even if bruised, browned by our scramble
   over the wall
with her screaming at us, threatening
   to call the police,
she who picked baskets-full without joy.

We trembled one time though, surprised
   by the old man,
her fragile father let out on his own
   who winked at us
finger at lips, and gave us apples
   burnished on his tweeds,
his sharp sweet apples snatched from the earth.

Fin de Siècle

Bright carcasses and red broad-aproned men
waltzed, whistling, about the scrubbed wood block.
Luminous tiles of emerald, cream and gold
clad walls and pillars. Offal shone on trays
embellished with crimped parsley, silver sage.
Mutton was crowned with paper butcher's lace.
A fountain played, tier to ceramic tier,
before the cashier's ledger-lined recess
and fed a sunken pool where rouged fish hung.
Resinous sawdust carpeted the flags.

The customers are smarter now than then
but frills have gone: my childhood's butcher's shop
is business-like, bleached as a hospital;
white tiles, white plastic trays, plate-glass, chrome-plate
and cling-filmed flesh like animal spare-parts,
the crashing till and clash of knife on steel
no longer softened by a fountain's plash.
Patrons no longer jostle naked flanks
nor do pigs sag on hooks, strain senseless snouts
to scents raised from the sawdust by their blood.

135

Minding Things

'You mind things; you'm observant I can see,'
you say, head down, walking your lane with me.
I am all eyes, pointing things out to you,
arms going like a gale-mazed scarecrow:
there, mole's morse tapped out in darkness
blebs your ground; there, new tenants in the trees;
or there, a fresh-dug earth bleeds your field-bank.
'Oh yes,' you say without looking, hands sunk
deep in pockets, 'that old oont's shiftin'.
They nest there reg'lar. Soon I'll snare his run.'
Your eyes-down is a blind. You mind each flare
and tic in your field-nerves, as a blind man
reads his own body-scape. I stare and stare.

Farrier's Dog

Here's one dog won't get under horse's hoofs;
he sits, haunched-up attention, by the forge,
belly like bellows and tooth-printed tongue.

His master heats and hammers soft pink iron,
chimes nail-holes through; dog blinks through parted air;
horse flicks its flank, sweats, lights a livid eye.

The man slaps its taut neck, hefts up its foot
against his thigh and with a quick knife pares
hoof-rind away; the dog whines silently.

The red shoe is by burning bedded in;
from out a thick gout of ammonia smoke
and thin steam spurting when the shoe is quenched

a mess of parings comes, kicked to the dog
who in crouched, greedy spasms gulps it down;
iron is hammered home, and the horse stamps.

Day of the Goat

Today the goat jumped on to my back.
Horns burn craters into my skull.
My eyes waste in their own heat.
My beard wags with greedy distaste.
I am full. I am hateful.
My makeshift bones begrudge
my belly's bulk. My head itches
to butt. I am out of joint.
I am tethered to a deep-sunk stake.
A massive chain drags my jaws back
to fouled grass. Objects of lust
flourish beyond its fullest extent.

Drouth End

The stream shrank, curdled in its bed;
cows, maddened, scoured salt flanks.

At last, huge thunder-rain struck
scents from the parched fields.

The river swelled, broached banks,
thick tree-boles breasted it,

all night it scaled the bridge piers,
by first light wet the arch.

Fish nestled in hoof-print,
cattle broke bounds through hedge,

for days trod more than they could cud,
hobbled on rot. Milk waned.

The Shrinkage Back

Leant at the glass
you touch your face.

Your skin is changeable,
it suffers with the cold,

the winters it sloughs off;
yet it is cared for both

by you with water
and by my bare hands.

Skins meet against the elements
and wear each other down,

the shrinkage back
to what our skins contain;

our bodies, changeable,
that will be changed.

Senses more deft than touch
feel for our glorious bodies.

Bird-lover

Despite the cold she stands
studying the blank place
where she had cast breadcrusts
and fat sliced small.

Nothing left in the snow
but a pricked arena
entered from all angles
by trailing claws

where the birds alighted.
Outside the circle is
nothing but her footsteps
to dent the day.

She has an appetite.
Despite the cold she stands
and absorbs the map of
her devotion.

Boy's Shadow
(for Tom Groves)

Friday, your father's body burned,
you saw the grey dust blow away.

Sunday, you danced beneath the sun
and made a new discovery –

your shadow – how you jumped, peered in
and twisted to escape the boy

you found was latched onto your limbs.
It chases you the more you fly

until you tire and tumble down
to meet the dark and with it lie.

An Accident of Love

Your time came. The cord cut
finally, not birth –
that head and body,
all four little limbs
– but amputation.

An accident of love
which you've survived;
a part of you, and more
a growth out of you both
cut off, outlived.

That is unbearable.
Still birth because
nothing moves that should.
What can he do but try
impossible comfort?

He too an amputee
asking, Oh where
my dear, where does it hurt?
The pain is sharpest in
what is not there.

To My Son

My son, this is for you, though
God alone knows where you are.
We worry about you and want you
to know that we wish you were here.

I wish you'd hear. Talking to you's
like less than talking to the dead,
but tonight I must; I cannot go,
although I'm tired of talking, to my bed.

Where we make love your mother lies alone;
where we ache for you in our joy
your mother's tears mourn you. I do it too
my way, for you or for your sister, boy.

The door is open where I come and go
for you to darken; there's a welcome here.
Till then, this is for you, though
God alone knows where you are.

Avebury Child

An exhumation under glass
set into the museum's floor:
shallow earth-bed, a window on
a child forty centuries dead;

skull like a fire-burst cooking-pot
askew on ribs like driftwood and
flexed legs like the broken shafts
of something with no known use.

A child watches this, head inclined
to it, person crouched on the brink,
while his parents move about him.

Their rooted child watches a child;
the glass untroubled by a breath
of wind, clear skin of a steep pond.

Stone Age

(for Jane Lees, Avebury)

In your dad's fields, megaliths grew like mushrooms
Big stones like planets hovered in deep meadow

Cows rubbed at elementary particles
orbiting your eccentric nucleus

Now you mock strangers who stretch dowsers' hands
to touch with arcane intimacy holy things

You smile at how – innocent of their potency
of neolithic physics and metaphysics –

you scaled them all, straddled them and slid down
knickers in holes, how your mum scolded you

A Dig Through Dust

I dream a dig through dust:
a pit I cannot tell how deep,
Sheol, the grave perhaps,
timber long since riddled to ash.
I scratch and sieve for goods;
ornaments, spindle-whorls and bones.

Find none. A post-hole then
whose tree and cross-tree raised a roof;
I comb the flinty ground
for sherds, grain, signs of the sacred
or profane, black layers
of occupation; and find none.

But for three Roman nails,
rust-cankered. Post-hole then, and grave.
Out of the dig's raised dust
a man – a gardener – appears
to set a seed in it.
Water, he says. I wake in tears.

BERNICIAN SONNETS

Holy Island

Sun fires the Priory of Lindisfarne.
A metalled, wrack-strewn fillet of sea-sand
scuffed, at the ebb, by feet of saints and kings
leads us to slits pierced by Scot-fearing eyes,
a shell upon the shade of Cuthbert's shrine.
Warm limbs like Cuddy's beads, tried more by wind
than dissolute clerks or sharp-prowed Vikings,
weather grainwise to bones, combs, traceries.

Wind fans the hair and dries the lips I kissed.
I want to tempt the tide until it laves
mainland from us; repel all grounded keels;
risk meeting Cuthbert, old misogynist
emerging from the mortifying waves
his feet warmed by salt tears and tongues of seals.

Durham

High above Wear as Wear's above the sea
we look for Cuthbert's shrine beneath grey flags;
his headless effigy clasps Oswald's head
behind the saintless eyes of Neville's screen.
Refugee bones found in the sanctuary
of incorrupt flesh and glorious rags
at Dissolution, two weeks' growth of beard;
and venerable Bede's thieved skeleton.

Half Church of God, half castle 'gainst the Scot.
Prisoners, after Dunbar, to keep warm
burnt all its wood except the painted clock:
a reckoning three centuries too late
re-wrote some deaths; each hacked-at Neville tomb
is sculpted meat upon a butcher's block.

Dunstanburgh

Stone limbs stand for the potency of fall.
Cheviot lays her dark declensions down,
whole castles grapple ground, pits lift their heads;
the territory tilts towards the shock
of wave on Whin Sill, whose grey columns, walls
make theatres for the tides to play, and drown
our lovely stutterings; strata are boards
thrust at the christened Farnes, the Nameless Rock.

If like doomed lovers we had leaned on wind,
heels bruising the romantic sod, I think
we must have slipped; but dwarfed by masonry,
sun-warmed like spartan grass, we stand our ground
and let aspiring ruins on the brink
cry Folly, folly, folly, tenderly.

PURBECK POEMS

Purbeck Progress

Salt mists creep on the sunlit hills
as if the sea beyond reclaimed
its own pure chalk whose calcined bone
under cropped grass is Purbeck's spine,
ocean's upswelling laid-down dead.

Below are clay-scapes, gravel troughs,
relicts of repetitious seas'
transgressions and retreats; the waste
acidic heath whose flagrant furze
like yeast, works in the sun's oven.

Furrows, like ripples in the rough,
struggle from farmsteads, and revert.
Seawards, ramparts raised on the chalk,
strip-lynchets, stones chart human tides
while mounds like sea-marks compass them.

Those barrows of trussed bones disperse
in mist up on the chilling ridge.
The humming heath lies undisturbed;
men settled on the sun-baked earth
that soon must break over their heads.

Tubal

Old hag, the stretch-marked heath, had commerce with
sprawled harbour; watermark, birth-mark, her kith
whose wildfowl kin ride on the wake of yachts.
Her warships, ferries, clay-barges, stone boats,

her passage-houses, ports and wharves are dead;
tracks are ripped up, causeways and piles plumb mud;
her streams drain into saltings, fertile leas
where salters' steam distilled brine's currency.

Where withy-weave was caulked with her white mire
and stone, bronze, iron age pots were born of fire,
today, like hair on hag-skin, pines conceal
steel tongues seeking her juices, her black oil.

Her rusty sphagnum bogs are running sores;
her holy stones are warts; tumuli, tumours;
deeper, close-ranked pine trunks scent dark clay-lanes
where men excise her pressing, secret organs.

Poised above open wounds, great diggers prey
upon her grey-blue, blue-black, iron-bruised clay;
as, coiled at clay-pool, the heron stabs down
among white lilies, jerks flesh from toad bone.

Hurdle

Causeway from sea to sea dividing corn from heather,
sheepwalk once; now herbage clots with bracken,
curdles round flinty skulls, claw-hold for windhover;
and ploughshares strike up sparks, bite to the bone.

Tracks trickle down dry valleys to their source
where water, gone to ground, springs out like nerves;
man's monuments are sapped, precarious,
slight punctuation on the ridgeway's curves.

Corfe Castle's gap-toothed stones seem disinterred
and midwived mounds bear bones with backs to death;
bound foetus-shapes waiting for flesh and blood;
so Purbeck's fractured spine backs on to heath.

It starts from splintered stack and faulted cliff
and stops where men dug in against the foe,
banks and last ditches now defended with
a wall of air founded on waves below.

High seas gnaw softly at the chalk beneath
tall ramparts where a torn crow tempts the wind,
unpinioned, lifts off into the gale's teeth
and leisurely flails backwards, deep inland.

Plough

The island's lap: submissive soils,
plush copse, nesh grass and furrows' grain
each cropped in its own season; ordered
between deep hedgerows, Domesday's skein
unravelling between the hills,

Unharnessed from their mill-races,
dwarf streams that once carved clays and quartz
drain inwards to the island's heart;
and weed-grown railway ballast skirts
the common's horse-grazed calluses.

The summer strikes its garish tents,
retires in tints of Swanage brick;
sea-port whose sweated stones resort
to fun, and winter in the wake
of fake arcadian amusements.

But wildfire is the west's weather;
guns' thunder above ancient tillage.
Nature corrupts the laid-out dead,
roots and vermin mine the village,
carrion stoop to the vole's crater.

Biddle

Black holes, stopped throats of stone; barren well-heads
– whose buttressed capstans groaned at drawing rock
up into daylight – sound successive beds
and teem with fossil dead of sea, swamp, lake.

Old mammals, dinosaurs' tread, crocodiles
congealed between the cliffstone's ammonites
and marble's burnishable snail-whorls.
Time, unmanned, in the rocks' mirror distorts.

Sea-walls and city streets, churches, headstones
excised, exported; here, still monuments of air
erected underground. Open-cast mines,
like pores, sweat rocks from rising strata:

an ancient virgin face at heart, composed
by wedge and biddle, stern chimes from quarr-shop.
Sea's tongues speak in hacked caverns, which no glazed
tallow-light or music now lick into shape.

Lanes founder beneath turf, and at cliff-edge
dry stone unpicked; man's strata, walls' web stutters
surf-wards, the plateau's net that, plucked, would dredge
a catch of crops, herds, flocks and stonecutters.

Drill

Limestone backs up inland; sublime viewpoints
supervise sea beyond deep seas of clay,
petrified, plundered swell; but carpeted
emerald and gold to the eye whose prey
is unspoilt beauty, nature out of joint.

Among the corn fox flaunts his flaming brush,
his earth the burning cliff whose brimstone breath
sours sea-mist; the grim shales' blackstone hoard
turned jet-like trinket on a flint-tooled lathe;
its fractions, gas-light, oil, tar, fertile ash.

Where small boats chart cement-stone's jagged hards
tarred pots net flesh in armour. Steened conduits
plumb the ground's wild water. Wire snares are laid
in tracks as lost as tramways to old adits.
Though leys from earth to quarry spurn man's roads,

both kinds in the keeper's mind intersect.
Prospecting eyes redraw the lines of sight;
the watchtower in decay, but at well-head
an iron donkey draws new tarmac to it.
Crude depths and refined distances connect.

*   *   *

Man, Ass & Tree

A seasoned tree
in a landscape
what water there
is is high cloud
going elsewhere

A man seated
on an ass is
making for it
for there's nothing
else in his eye

But ochre dust
rocks and in his
twin saddlebags
the sharp tools of
a carpenter

     *   *   *

The dead tree is
not thunderstruck
not gaunt it is
a tuft of twigs
on a dry stalk

The man speaks to
his ass If in
its shade there is
grass you shall graze
if fruit I'll eat

That some way off
they come nearer
they come to it
he bites the words
off his tongue

     *   *   *

Needlessly he
tethers his ass
sees how termites
riddle the bark
with their soft life

Watches the ants
clamber his boots
and how they shine
on dust-dull hoofs
how his ass kicks

The ass whites its
eye at the moon
there is no wind
only in the
man's skull twigs rasp

*   *   *

In the morning
there is no grass
water a sip
and tack a bite
for the good man

By its tether
he tugs one eye
tight to the trunk
the other blinks
at a distance

Lashes the neck
to the tree's rind
the leash bites deep
but the heart's sound
he cuts the throat

*   *   *

Blood oils his hands
slips the knot he
slits the corpse's
coat from penis
to lower lip

Now the man weeps
sorry sorry
presses hands down
a round embrace
shrubs the hide off

Shucks the sack of
luminous lites
that splits vivid
but so near void
not much to clean

*   *   *

Lopped twigs like masts
fly flags of flesh
out of ant reach
intestines shrink
hide stinks and cures

A fire burns bark
in a circle
of flints whose skins
darken bones blanch
meat cooks and smokes

By the naked
bole the man squats
works precisely
with a small file
sets the saw's teeth

*   *   *

He sets the saw
to the heart wood
its rasp ripples
away in gusts
there's no echo

All this takes time
in the fine grain
paring warping
in the fire's heat
all this making

A kind of box
box with curves a
hollow body
with certain holes
shaft like a neck

      *   *   *

With sticks the man
twists ass's gut
the fragile hose
thins stringily
wiry and strong

He sweats bending
a stick a spring
tense with taut hairs
from the hide's tuft
his slender bow

Anchored strings stretch
wound with pegs up
straining between
body and neck
nervy creature

      *   *   *

There's nothing here
with which to know
how sound it is
how big in space
bass violin

An instrument
is enough now
for the man who
burnishes it
with his hands' oil

He packs his tools
with love and plucks
the thing trims it
plucks bows it speaks
the thing is tuned

      *   *   *

The fire cackles
under the moon
the man seated
on the tree-bole
cloaked in ass-skin

Calmly simply
like a madman
drags the bow to
and fro the air
in the thing sings

The ground of him
a stump of veins
rooted in rock
but the heart wood
wakes in his hands

    * * *

His cavities
his emptiness
resound the pulse
all his nerve blurs
under the bow

Tugged and let go
so quick high low
spills pitch thickens
marrow sinew
oh tugged let go

Till the man groans
leans in grows in
flows into night
fills it the stars
shriek the ground quakes

    * * *

So far away
a pack of dogs
senses something
sent on the wind
and makes for it

Tatters of meat
cold ash fired flints
skin rags and bones
carcase of wood
termites and ants

Saddlebags and
silence that's all
they find under
shrieking stars on
the quaking ground

Jerusalem Zoo

They shall not hurt or destroy in all my holy mountain
ISAIAH 11.9

In Jerusalem they are forcing God's hand.
Cages, high fences enable paradise
inside them; or will, when what the Zoo has planned
is brought to pass with all the stoic purpose
of Dispersion gathered to possess the land.

In Cage One, strange bedfellows, lambs with the wolf;
in Two, leopard and kids. Rank fur rubs fleece.
In Three and Four, the lion preens himself,
the bear walks on hind feet; they nuzzle grass
with skittish comrades, the fatling and the calf.

Eden behind bars. Replenished earth subdued.
Pilgrim and sightseer, Arab and Jew will press
wide eyes and lenses at Isaiah construed
with exact pedantry. To haste Messias
a baby in Cage Five crawls on the asp's brood,

a weaned child puts his hand on the adder's den.
Apart, at night, the prey chew cud. Predators
rend red meat, gorge in the old tradition.
So is the new day filled with docile creatures
and, to be realistic, model children.

Small cages. Man still at large, who paused to weep
over Jerusalem, astride a young ass
rode over strewn garments, crowd's applause, their hope
pinned to a cross. He must repeat that progress,
bars must burst, and the millennium escape.

Making History
(for Charles Willson Peale)

Upstate New York with thunder threatening rain
and your broad canvas stretched to capture it:
your workmen, waterlogged in a deep pit
where but for a great treadmill's sweat they'd drown,
spade mud by stages, sifting it for bone.
Aside, posed gentlemen and ladies wait
subdued as at a funeral of state:
the *Disinterment of the Mastodon*.

Bones made articulate in your dry rooms,
ribs out of Union clay restored by science
nerved by the lightning's stampede through the trees;
a resurrection for the dime museums
fleshed by your Old World brush: the renaissance
that heaves the ponderous New World from its knees.

Sebastian

The arrows' incisions ooze prettily
and not too much. The pale still-upright flesh
an officer of the Praetorian Guard.
Flèched shafts point backwards to a firing-squad.
Sentenced for faith in Christ, but suffering
shamelessly and the painters enjoying it
too much, suggesting God thrives, as they thrive
on paint, on blood. God nurses his wounds.

Sebastian left for dead, but Castulus'
widow heals him. His wounds not stigmata:
they shut and stop leaking. He witnesses
till Diocletian says barbs were too good.
Cudgels suit. Cudgel him to death. The squad
takes cudgels in both hands, makes sure this time.
This is not pretty. Renaissance painters
don't choose this. Man, unrecognisable.

Sisyphus in Love

Dark-veined limestone, this woman
whose mass he manhandles uphill;
her rounds, her clefts, her pale fossil,
he loves them all. Near the summit
his whole flesh bruises her stone,
breathes against her for brief respite.

Then she speaks to him of ocean,
of what she and the sea have spawned;
her rocky arms go around
his neck, over, over they roll,
his heels graze the green hill again
and again, his bones grind to meal.

And again, each time he loves her.
The fossil inside her holds tight,
won't break from its shell, nor plummet
them quite to the sea. Ocean:
he stumbles, scrambles, shoves her
uphill to hear of it again.

DOMINGUS

for Martin Ware & Barry Anderson

Domingus

Dear friend Domingus – legendary ogre
of the Devil's House, said to boast
vast secret cellars, dankest dungeons
infernally furnished, and tunnels
reputed to insinuate the town's roots
– Domingus wearied. Townswomen skirted
his great walls on the street's far side,
shawls cowled to shield averted faces;
foolhardy men peered over, and the boldest
tearaways, deaf to their elders' pleas,
flung echoing taunts through chinks
in his doors, 'Strike us dead, Domingus!'

Wearied with infamy, Domingus opened
his portals to the public at no fee.
His alms box filled on the third day,
then twice each day for two weeks.
Kindly Domingus guided them round
parts of the house. They looked on it
and him, once-evil hermit, and went away.
Now no one comes. Women walk openly by,
men mock at the poor old bastard
and every last urchin tosses rocks
through the grills, pisses on his walls.
Dear friend Domingus works in peace.

Seed of the Town

Domingus paced large on the mound
lost in his plans. (The old recount
such memories that youth cannot contain.)
Trees were uprooted, earth dishevelled,
stone hewn from a green quarry and
ferried, at some cost, down river;
the river that then ran clean.
Men died also in the digging.

The fabric grew out from him
with the radiance of raw stone.
It was glorious: his costume.
It was impregnable: his armour.
It guarded machination:
his arches of bone, his cranium.

Later they called it Devil's House.
Ferns, saplings spring from the quarry's wounds.
The river silts with dung; bright algae bloom.
The House corrodes with liverwort and lichen.
Domingus scurries there for days on end.

Flowers for Domingus

Domingus lives an absence.
Dull footfalls on his pavements,
graffiti on his grey walls gnaw
at what Nature abhors.

Death's pains and birth's quick pangs,
dumb tears and quiet love-songs
are innocent of power,
confined within closed doors.

But when passion is public
on the wind, when streets are black
with mourning, then, if he needs
tears' luxury, his stone heart bleeds.

Fate moves and has her season.
But he will invent no reason
why he hears gay laughter burst
with song and dance at every feast.

Flowers in his arid garden
these, blown in the wind. He claims none
but must needs smile as if in sleep;
weep as an ancient child must weep.

Domingus and the Bitch

At risk to himself Domingus
scavenges a bitch from her suitors.
His gates close on a mob of dogs.

Roused, she snarls in his teeth. He smiles.
She fouls the flagstones, bloodies his court
and mounts him in her heat.

Ardour amuses him: he tempts it;
tempts her, wins her with the choicest meat
and oversees her appetite.

Sated, she rolls, sprawls on her back;
with burnished boots he treads her paps;
later she sleeps, jaws in his lap.

Artfully he indulges her.
Love comes to that. And this, his temper
on a fuse, her frigid whimper.

Her whimper as, full fed and watered,
he kicks her through his gates, in vain
to squat and piss against the town.

Vort

Here, in the dusty courtyard,
dressed in rough shirt, hide sandals
(his mask and apron safe inside
folded like ceremonials)
Vort stands and swings at flotsam.
Brats fight, and women chatter
over baskets in the sun.
Sweat varnishes taut muscle, scatters
as the honed axe head
chimes deep into the block.
Rehearsal here. And firewood.

From every sighing stroke
kindling flies clean into the sand.
This is a craftsman's iron love.
Here, squealing children understand
the mercy of a tempered nerve.

Vort and Domingus

Masked, good Vort hides himself
and bares a brutish arm.
He is the merest instrument
who knows Domingus' name.
The justices invoke it.
Strong as an ox, they say,
and peaceable, sacrificed
to a higher will that cleaves
the necks of insurrectionists,
Vort spits upon his calluses.
The justices wear scarlet gloves.

Sometimes Domingus watches,
hears the wilful last confession,
clenches his fist and, at the last
involuntary convulsion,
speaks his awful name; then looks
to read it in his wounded palm.

Kennan

Kennan, conceived of rape, died at Vort's hand.
He preached that power was bastard spawn,
his very flesh the proof, cursed before Heaven;
saw lust in justices' and merchants' eyes
and swore to avenge the fear that groaned
and grew with him beneath his mother's gaze.

He gathered to him in the lowest taverns
the weavers, tillers, foundrymen who fanned
their discontents to white-hot blaze,
wove shirts of steel and forged an iron seed
which was to burst and prise apart the stones
that usury raised up upon men's need.

The merchants built; he craved a martyr's crop
and cried his message in the market.
Restrained by officers at law, was stopped
at last by Vort's swift blade. *They* did not
prune a dream, or geld a vision –
righteously they defaced fraudulent coin.

The Death of Kennan

Committed to the earth
he parted it, whose dust and stone
honed him to glittering.
His headstone was an icon,
and in his furrow's depths
celebrants of his mourning
sowed perennial wreaths;
tears watered them, their song
awaited spring.

Tears of the few are too few
and the frost, the wordless frost
of each staid fearful citizen
too long freezes the ear.
Songs despair. Kennan is best
forgotten, Devil's House is there
and this, his cornerstone
is one, and overgrown with weed
that speaks of treason.

Domingus, unmoved by the dead,
grows old and in his fashion mourns
a barren season.

168

Domingus Emerges

Domingus grows alone; airless
in sullen rooms, yearns breath
of his town, stench of coarse speech
on his face. Domingus, great one,
grows faithless in his solitude.

Disguised, he surfaces somewhere
into thronged streets, and revels there
in silence, among common men.
Often he purchases small trinkets
only to chuck away. Mainly

he watches. Perhaps a child pipes
'There's Domingus.' But then, they point
at strangers and speak his name,
while he, snug in his lair, sits
breathing deep, sated with due contempt.

Domingus Spoils for a fight

Domingus plays like the old gods;
truant from his haunt, in rags
he begs downtown, beseeches
men for bread and coin, searches
their eyes with a god's gaze.
Refused, he smiles on their hard wills,
thrills with their righteousness.
Obliged with an open purse, he scans
a hoard of hopes, scavenges
for guilt. Domingus plunders paupers;
thieves custom from flower-hawkers
outside sanatorium and graveyard.

Back in his house, himself again,
he chucks the coppers one by one
through his bars: largesse to the young
who hoard for nothing but themselves.
He chuckles, seeing how they must
spoil, brawl and fly free, blooded
knuckles clutching a coin's dull rust.

Domingus' Relics

To have travelled light was to have settled
powerless. That vein, bled costly
from its rock, refined and cast,
was borne down by his retinue
and laid up in his haunt's bowels.
Loadstone for lust; its virtue
in the wasted sweat from which it was distilled.
The bedrock of the Devil's House.

Boys in their paradise
barter pebbles and fools' gold.
Merchants see usury enough in silver.
Townsmen spend copper coin.
All dream of the real thing.

With awe and hate Domingus squats among it.
Gold serves him. He is possessed.
The vault holds them secure.
He fears no pillager but worms
and dreams of dying there; his vault, his element
and all his haunt falling to dust
with him. He sees the townsmen
prize and preach the virtue of
his bleached and venerable bones!

Domingus Dead

'Domingus dead!' The cry abounds
in all the town, and draws it tight:
a knot around his blackened haunt.
Still chastened by his shadowy cast
old women's eyes turn to it. Blindly
the children chant. Astrologers
and archivists find quick employ.
Gossip flows gleefully in taverns;
later, in lonely streets, men sicken.

Him, dead. The rumour's genesis
is shrouded still. The wise ones
doubt it, and are somehow glad.
Smiling a deathly smile, Domingus
blesses thrice all resurrection men.

Domingus' Changes

At dawn Domingus seems to wake. He warms.
There is a day. And how he poses for it;
views himself upright in his maze of stone
amazed at what he's weighty with.

Stone spaces sigh with night-soiled breath,
nightmares are drowned by his blood's rhythm;
the same, always the same. And yet
he cannot name what this consists of.

This same two: scrap over differences.
Willing his walls' confinement, as of right,
himself butts at his skull, to break from that.
He poses; sees what passions fit him best.

To no avail; for what grows in him is
Domingus, changeable, unknown; although at dusk
nestled in barren stone, they wrestle close
till dawn, the one thriving upon the other's dust.

Domingus Deafened

The raw sun burns above the town
that draws itinerants to it
not to him. His chamber like an oven,
towers like stacks. As if through smoke
hears merryandrews, mountebanks,
incorrigible preachers, all their pains
like tingling at his far nerve ends.

Domingus loosely framed about his bones
squints through a skylight's murk,
'Oh God, what must I do?' and strains
to hear the silence that descends.

The air is full of thunder that won't break.
Something soft in him slips, aborts
with tears not blood; embers are fanned.
He hears, like the wind's hand against a pane,
words pressing at his ear, peace and disquiet:
'Turn, turn again.' Domingus deafened.

*   *   *

Riddles for Jack

1

I am dark and copious
a place to be born

On my floor earth sifts
with the seasons' husks

Winds dry and pollen-thick
stir them, shake my doors

What the tillage crops
is pitched into my dark

Barred, braced against harvest
my storm-timbers groan

I am a hold, a hoard
a made pod ripe in winter

Plunder me then
but know that I exact

Strict tithes for rats, mice
all my familiars

2

I am sun-bleached, rain-washed
My brick and stone breed lichen

My walls warm from within
My windows light on bounty

Inventories add and subtract
pots, emblems, beds, live cargo

My doors open and shut
I am a passage and a halt

My furniture, my linen
suffer private weathers

I am well and hardly used
My stone face does not shift

But what is born in me
is at length borne out

Blinded by boards I sink
Midden in a rife plot

   3

Unlived-in, not aloof
I am a place apart

My door's weight gives
into soft sainted light

Garnished with flowers
my crevice of worked stone

Rich seam, bronze chime
stones dwindle and plumb heaven

Be still, refined as gold
in the flame's stance

Plate that sustains sparse meals
the faithful's striving

Know that when they are gone
I am a sighing shell

And in my yard
nothing but standing stone

4

Abandoned now I am
an ocean to myself

I am deep down, agape
solicit stones and coins

My mouth holds its reply
my bowels water

Full of rumour I return
no glib reflection

Come gather at my rim
glimpse my stare's spark

I'll not fall from my pit
nor overstep the eye's sill

I am all settling, seepage
Wishes silt in my loins

Fear them, follow them
My pure juice will scour you clean

Holding

My neighbour's legs lend him such scant support
he cannot tend his plot, but farms it out.
I stake and chain goats there, tripping across
footings of sheds abandoned to the grass
where once his girlish sows suckled their young.
Where spring greens thrived the goats graze arcs among
his pleasurable thistles. He and his shame
move painfully within his living-room.

Our smallholdings adjoin a farm
whose fields fall to the valley and then climb
over the spine of the next hill. But greed
extends itself, even confined to bed
as that old farmer is. His sheets
are paper-thin; between them he spawns writs
and counter-writs: actions that he can take.
His sons and men do all the dirty work.

When they beat bounds it is to beat them back,
my neighbour says. Last time they struck
they staked new fence two yards beyond the bound
and quickly felled the trees that stood their ground.
The case drags on. Keep your eyes skinned, he says.
So I patrol, alert to all forays
that even cows and blackbirds mount against
our wire, beaded with knots of rust.

A tractor, trailer, load of fence-posts trussed
with barbs, and four young men raise dust,
arrive. I warn my neighbour. Stare them out.
They laugh, begin offloading, but stop short:
he takes to his old paths unerringly
and breaks a shotgun over his frail knee.
They load, and leave; sheepish, I too retire
as old men join: one in his bed of power,
one planted in his plot with a cocked gun,
and open ground, crisp acreage in between.

Terrorist

I know that I am beautiful
in my own beech woods,
my brush over the beechmast;
my bark out-bugles men.

Ah, to their shameful dog-packs,
the nervy beasts they ride
in their crude coats, they are kind.
I would bite the hand.

At dusk now, unearthed, soft-foot
through my own beech woods,
through grass, I thread a route;
reaching their wire, I breach it.

Here are their birds, cooped, clipped;
their nicely nurtured chicken
that one by one they cull.
They are kind to be cruel.

I'm a beast in this place
with no escape. I don't know
if it's for that, from lust,
or to teach men what is just

that I harry, hunt birds
bred in fear in this cell,
that I kill, voiding blood
and feathers and untouched dead.

My bark out-bugles men,
my brush over the beechmast;
in my own beech woods
I know that I am beautiful.

Watering Place

From pastureland I once dropped down
through a steep wood to where the sun
stopped in deep leaves before it lit
the floor, though a stream gathered it
and drew me, straying child, toward
music that light and water made...
I found the carcass of a ram
fallen across it, a queer dam;
dead weight, soft fleece of washing wool,
grub-addled matter in its shell.

With adult sense there on the brink
I dared to stoop, upstream, and drink.
But since, wading in sleep, I've fled
headlong, parched, sick, hoping to tread
water where nothing died, a source,
untarnished tarn where sheer falls slice
into iced water, mirrored heaven.
I'll not dip there awake. As then
I must cup hands close to the rot,
upstream, just, where the water's sweet.

A Farmer

A farmer here for close on sixty years,
it's true the last ten haven't seen him near
so much as the barn. In the front parlour
trussed up and baled in his invalid's chair
yet still disdaining rugs and pyjamas
he reaps with his tongue, recounts the pre-war
price of corn, or his first horsedrawn ploughshare
and with a fingernail white as new flour
cuts in his russet corduroy trousers
as fine a furrow as he could wish for.

179

Best Bone

'I haven't often brewed up tea for two
since he passed on,' she smiles. I'm an impostor
posing here; a thief, that I shall have to
take myself away. 'My friends have gone,
I wonder why I stay to plague the young

like you, it was so good of you to come.'
Her eye is fragile and her voice is thin.
The pottery is stout, a gay design
absurdly garish in her dim front room,
'It brightens up my mausoleum.'

She smiles again. I'd have expected
pastel porcelain that had survived
her years, perhaps her mother's. Instead
we drink from this. The fine stuff is displayed
behind glass in the corner cupboard.

The teacups there, some whole, some chipped or crazed,
gather no dust, that once were filled and raised
from this same lace to smiling lips of friends
whose grins now widen as the flesh recedes.
'What remains I want preserved.' She reads

the makes from memory, 'Best bone, but their
fragility and mine don't go together,
my sight is bad, I'm clumsy. I remember
mother beat me when I chipped her china.'
Her frail jaw juggles with soft laughter,

her knuckles whiten as she lifts the cup's
thick rim, so gently, to her parched blue lips,
steam clouds her eyes, and gently, as she sips,
age beats the living daylights out of her.

Two poems for Lily Tilsley,
my grandmother, born 1872

A Proper Vanity

Her hair glistened in sunlight
and her hands, knotted and frail at rest,
unpinned it fluently, unloosed
the braided white, combed and caressed
the skein unfurling to her waist.

Miraculous that it should root
between a skull and skin pared
to a bare necessity, spared
this last grace. Her wasted face
fell into sensuous repose,

properly vain, till her grim hands
set to plait up each straying strand;
her glory, weight of womanhood
laboriously dressed, braided
and bound; its business, to persist.

October 12th 1972

The box we bear is cold
and surprisingly light.

One I love should weigh more.

NOTES

The Dimensions of Cleveland, 3 (16): The story goes that young James Cook was sacked from his apprenticeship to the grocer/draper in Staithes for stealing a South Sea Company shilling from the till. He went to Whitby and joined ship. The Tourist Board now sells a swathe of Cleveland/North Yorkshire as 'Captain Cook Country'.

Iron and Steel (14) and **Flying** (17): 'Bords' are spaces excavated between pillars left to support the ironstone mine's roof.

Richard Leycolt (20): Three Dorset alum workers who went to North Yorkshire were Richard Leycolt, Richard Southworth and Richard Atwater, one of whom – probably Leycolt – was the 'Black Dick' referred to by Sir Arthur Ingram in 1619.

Young Lucie Comes to Tea (25): Lucie Duff Gordon would become famous for her *Letters from Egypt* (1865), but at the age of 13, in 1834, she performed her favourite party trick at the house of Frederick North, MP, in Hastings.

The Concertina in Its Cage (28): The medium Daniel Dunglas Home was satirised by Robert Browning in 1864, but authenticated by scientist Sir William Crookes in 1871. At his death some tiny one-octave mouth organs were discovered among his effects.

Spirit from the Forest (34): The bitonal phrase for 'white man' in the drum language of the Congo means 'spirit from the forest'.

Lament (34): The Lingala word 'kwanga' means manioc bread.

The Leaves' Audible Smile (37): An English version of Fernando Pessoa's poem of 27 November 1932:

For Pero Moniz, who died at Sea (38): Commissioned in 2000 for European Poems on the Underground, this is a version of Luís de Camões' sonnet, first published in 1598:

La Virgen con el niño escribiendo en un libro (39): The painting of this title by Luis de Morales 'el Divino' (1509-86) is in the Museu de Bellas Artes, Valencia, Spain.

P(r)aying for Dinner (43): Gold currency minted for the Christian king of Mercia, Offa (757-96), were imitations of coins of Caliph al-Mansur and reproduced Arabic script as if it were mere decoration.

In Chittlehampton Churchyard (51). The first part of this poem was published in my collection *The Stubborn Forest*, in memory of my father who died in 1979. The second part is for my mother who died in 2000.

Wedding Song (53): A song commissioned in 2000 for the marriage of two dancers, Daniel Burnham and Dawn Fuhrman, and set to music for singers and chamber ensemble by the composer David Everett.

Dom Sebastião, King of Portugal (69): After *D. Sebastião, Rei de Portugal* by Fernando Pessoa. Dom Sebastião died in battle with the emperor of Morocco at Ksar-el-Kebir in 1578. Tradition has it that he, 'the one-that-is', will return as saviour of the Portuguese.

Wormwood (87): I wrote this poem after hearing an item about the aftermath of the Chernobyl disaster on BBC Radio 4's *From Our Own Correspondent*. Some mischief was made with the story by the right-wing press, denounced by the Bishop of Kiev. However the report I had heard was subsequently confirmed and I checked the meaning of 'chernobyl' in Ukrainian (thanks to Karen Hayes and Andrew Lachowitz).

Bernician Sonnets (145-46): *Durham*. 995-99, Cuthbert's remains brought to Durham from Lindisfarne; 1346, the battle of Neville's Cross; 1650, the battle of Dunbar.

Purbeck Poems (148-53): The Isle of Purbeck is washed by the sea to east and south; it is separated from the rest of Dorset by Poole Harbour and the River Frome to the north, and almost cut off to the west by a small stream called Luckford Lake. The poems are ways of looking at a landscape of extraordinary geological compression and great beauty, dense with the outcropping of history and of long, intensive exploitation. The titles of the poems are my names for Purbeck's main geological divisions.
   Tubal – the heathy Bagshot Beds which stretch from the harbour to the hills. They are underlain by lenses of ball-clay and by the largest onshore oilfield in Britain. A tubal is a claygetter's curved spade.
   Hurdle – the range of chalk hills which bisects the island; a barrier, or hurdle, with a gap defended by Corfe Castle, and a ridgeway upon which shepherds herded their flocks and folded them within hurdles.
   Plough – the fertile Wealden Clays of the Corfe Valley, lying between the hills and the limestone plateau, with Swanage Bay at one end and Tyneham, abandoned to Army manoeuvres, at the other.
   Biddle – the plateau of Cretaceous Purbeck and Portland Beds exploited in both pits and opencast workings. The northern seams are of "marble", while massive freestone was dug from cavernous cliff-quarries on the treacherous south coast. A biddle is a stonecutter's heavy hammer.
   Drill – The Kimmeridge Clays and Shales of Chapman's Pool, Brandy Bay and the Golden Bowl. Site of Romano-British and subsequent shale industries. The title refers to Purbeck's first oil-wells, sunk here in the 50s.

Jerusalem Zoo (160): Plans for Jerusalem Zoo were announced in *International Zoo News* and reported in the *Sunday Times* by Celia Haddon.

Making History (161): Charles Willson Peale (1741-1827) was a saddler, scientist, inventor and painter, important in the development of cultural identity in the U.S. His painting, *Disinterment of the Mastodon*, hangs in the Peale Museum, Baltimore.

INDEX OF TITLES & FIRST LINES

Index of titles and first lines

(Titles are shown in italics, first lines in roman type.)